GHOSTS

and

MYSTERIES

OF THE

OLD WEST

True accounts of New Mexico
and the Old West

by
Bob L'Aloge

illustrations by
David Kwiecinski

with
Marquita Peterson

Yucca Tree Press

First Printing   October 1990.
Revised Edition   September 1991.
Second Printing   August 1994

Cover design by Janie Matson and Bob L'Aloge.

Library of Congress Cataloging in Publication Data

L'Aloge, Bob

  Ghosts and Mysteries of the Old West: True Accounts of New Mexico and the Old West.

    1. Southwest United States - History.
      2. New Mexico Territory - History.
      I. Bob L'Aloge. II. Title

Library of Congress Card Catalog Number: 91-066180
ISBN 0-9622940-5-5

Illustrations by David Kwiecinski with Marquita Peterson

This book is dedicated to my son Joshua L'Aloge
and to the recognition of God in all humanity.

Happy Trails

for

Sarah

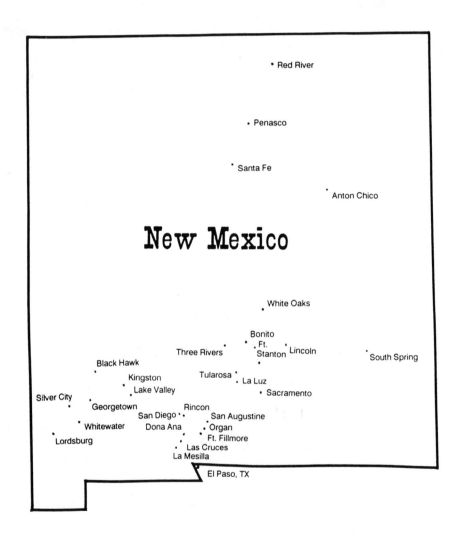

Towns and camps mentioned in the following stories.

Table of Contents

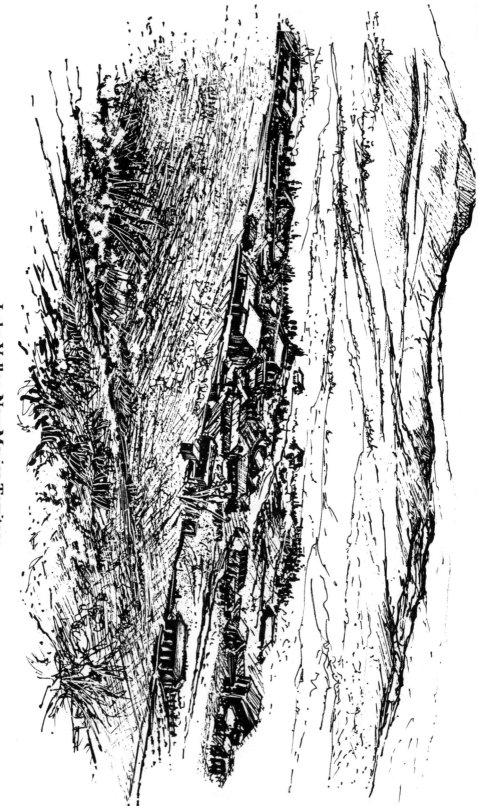

Lake Valley, New Mexico Territory

Ghosts and Mysteries of the Old West

Ghosts and mysteries are as much a part of the Old West as were cowboys, Indians, settlers, Winchesters and saloons. Yet we seldom hear of such things when reading about the adventures of those days.

"The American West remains a land of mystery and intrigue filled with spirits. . .who tamed the new frontier and who still haunt this beautiful but rugged land today," writes Earl Murray in *Ghosts of the Old West*.[1]

These vignettes follow ghosts and mysteries throughout the New Mexico Territory and the West. They are about ordinary people, and a few extra-ordinary ones, and give us a glimpse into the romance, excitement and adventure of the previous century.

The 'Ghost of the Double Eagle Restaurant' takes place in the small New Mexico town of La Mesilla.[2]

The building, once a residence but now a restaurant, was built in 1849 and is located on the east side of the Mesilla town plaza. During the Civil War a young man named Armando lived in the home. No doubt he was a handsome and dashing young man and captured the fancy of many a young girl. One particular girl was a housemaid named Inez.

The two struck up more than a friendship and were soon involved in a lusty affair.

People being what they are in the small towns of even today, gossip soon spread, and, no doubt, grew beyond reality. Disgrace was brought to the family. This caused Armando's mother to take his life with a knife.

Ghosts and Mysteries

Shortly after Armando's death, a skirmish took place in the plaza outside the house. Fate directed one of the bullets to Inez' heart and the young lady died. Now, according to believers, these two lovers roam the building at their leisure. Their favorite room is the Carlotta Room.

"I think they're having more fun now than when they were alive," Laura told the author during an interview at the Double Eagle Restaurant on October 24, 1989. "I was tending bar one evening. Suddenly about 70 or 80 glasses went tumbling off the back shelf. Luckily only three of them broke."

Laura seems a sensible young lady with eyes which shine like new china. One would think it hard for such an intelligent young lady to believe in ghosts. Yet, her many experiences while working at the restaurant have made her a believer.

Inez' and Armando's ghosts have been known to rearrange table settings, turn lights on and off, cause wear and tear to the furniture, and even pull the hair of one skeptical waitress. A present-day photograph of Inez' ghost presently hangs in the Carlotta Room.

The second story is a mystery and took place in Georgetown, New Mexico [now a ghost town]. The date was January, 1890 and it is called the "Cowboy With No Name."[3]

The weather was somewhat chilly that morning when an unknown cowboy rode into the booming mining town of Georgetown. His first thought was to get a drink of 'redeye' to warm his blood. Giving action to the thought, he rode over to one of the town's saloons, dismounted, tied his horse to the hitching rail, and stepped inside.

"Give me a whiskey," he demanded of the bartender. His order was filled. He quickly downed the drink and immediately ordered another. One drink followed another and soon the cowboy felt the results of the whiskey.

He became irate, took out his sixgun and "began taking pot shots at citizens." The town marshal, summoned to the scene, made an unsuccessful attempt to arrest the cowboy.

Finally, with the aid of several town citizens, the marshal made another attempt. This time he succeeded.

Taking the prisoner to the jailhouse, "the officers were met by a mob of masked men." These angry citizens forcibly took custody of the prisoner, dragged him to the nearest tree in the center of town, put a rope about his neck, and strung him up.

This still did not satisfy the mob. Several pulled out sixshooters and started to take pot shots at the dangling body.

Later that day, the body was hauled down and buried in the local cemetery. "The victim's identity was never known, nor did it matter. He had broken the law and had paid for his crimes."

The identity of this cowboy still remains a mystery. No one knew if he had any relatives or loved ones somewhere awaiting his return. No one ever will.

The story, 'The Ghost of Elizabeth Polly' took place outside of New Mexico. Because of its relevance it deserved to be included.[4]

In the mid-1860's, Ephraim and Elizabeth Polly traveled the Smokey Hill River country. Ephraim was a sutler who brought supplies and dry goods to the various forts and outposts along the Fort Hays-Fort Dodge trail. Falling in love with the Kansas countryside, Ephraim and Elizabeth decided to settle down in Fort Hays.

Many times Elizabeth was seen walking the peaceful bluffs outside the fort area. Sundown was her favorite time of day and she strolled the area at her pleasure, "her bonnet fastened tightly and her blue dress moving in the wind."

In 1867, a cholera epidemic broke out around the Fort Hays region. Records of old Fort Hays document that Ephriam Polly was a hospital steward during that cholera outbreak. Elizabeth was not mentioned, but that was not unusual.

During the epidemic, Elizabeth came down with cholera while tending the dying soldiers. On her death bed she made Ephraim agree to bury her "on the bluffs above the fort."

After her military funeral, they discovered the soil on the bluffs was too rocky to permit the digging of a grave, so Elizabeth was buried at the foot of the bluff.

Fort Hays residents erected a statue to her loving memory. But more than a statue reminds the citizens of Hays, Kansas that Elizabeth Polly once roamed her beloved hillsides.

Sightings of her ghost date back as far as 1917 and she has been seen by several respectable citizens, including a police officer who saw her in 1959.

"She was there! I saw her, I tell you. She was there," the officer repeated over and over to back-up officer Bob Maxwell when he arrived at the scene a few minutes later.

3

The 'Disappearance of Cherokee Jim Bowman' took place in New Mexico Territory in 1881.[5]

The role played by Black men and women in the history of the Old West is only now being researched and reported. One such Black man was Cherokee Jim Bowman. His story is very short because of a lack of details about him.

In the year 1881, Cherokee Jim "discovered a rich silver float in the Bullard's Peak district at the north end of the Burro Mountains."

The town of Black Hawk, New Mexico (now a ghost town) developed around Bowman's find. Black Hawk was about sixteen miles east of Silver City. For three years the town boomed and flourished. Residents built cabins, opened stores, and saloons served rotgut whiskey to miners for outrageous prices. Many a man became rich. When the mine played out the people drifted away.

What about Cherokee Jim Bowman?

No one knows whether he made any money off his find. He simply vanished somewhere in the hills of New Mexico and nothing more was heard of him. Nor is it known if he had any family. Perhaps no one will ever know.

A practical joke is the theme of the next mystery of the Old West. It took place in the present-day ghost town of Red River, New Mexico shortly before 1900. This is the 'Mystery Over Bitter Creek.'[6]

Flash floods were dangerous occurrences to the tiny mining town of Red River and were probably feared more than an Apache attack. Miners and storekeepers stayed constantly on the alert for news of an oncoming body of water which might wash away their property or themselves.

One spring day in 1899, three unknown cowboys rode down from the hills and into Red River. Their first stop was a saloon "that was built on piles over Bitter Creek." The creek ran through the heart of town. These three fun-loving cowboys, probably broke and down on their luck, related to the saloonkeeper how they'd just come into town ahead of a flash flood. The flood was headed directly for the town and would probably wipe out the saloon.

They assured the proprietor there was nothing to do but pack what he could carry and immediately flee. Within a matter of minutes they succeeded in scaring off the owner who took

4

with him his Winchester and two bottles of the best whiskey in the house.

What did these cowboys do next? They sat down at one of the poker tables and drank from the many whiskey bottles left behind by the saloonkeeper. After drinking their fill, and knowing the proprietor would soon return, they loaded the remaining whiskey into their saddlebags and made a hasty departure from Red River, New Mexico.

Finally, realizing there was no flash flood coming, the proprietor returned to find his shelves emptied of his whiskey supply. He immediately notified the town marshal. Nothing was ever done. The three cowboys were never brought to justice for their theft and practical joke. Instead, these mysterious cowboys rode off into the pages of history – unknown but not forgotten.

'The Ghost of Lt. Hodgson' began on a hot summer day, June 25, 1876. The location was the Little Big Horn where General George A. Custer, the Indian butcher, made his last stand.[7]

The familiar story of the Battle of Little Big Horn will not be repeated, except for the role played by Lt. Hodgson.

Five miles from where Custer and his men died, another battle took place on that memorable day. It involved Major Marcus Reno. Their fight lasted throughout the day and into the next. Reno and his men were getting 'their backsides kicked.' Major Reno lost control of his men who made a disorderly retreat across the Little Big Horn River and into the surrounding hills.

A short time later, a command under Capt. Fred Benteen joined Reno and his remaining men. Benteen found the scene one of blood, madness, and hysterical disorder. Throughout the day, soldier after soldier fell wounded or dead under the Indians' continual onslaught. The stench of blood and death hung heavily in the quiet aftermath of battle.

Present that day was a young Second Lieutenant, Benjamin H. Hodgson. He was of average build, closely trimmed brown hair, dark eyes, and a drooping handlebar mustache. He appeared to be in his early twenties. Hodgson was assigned to Company B of the famous Seventh Cavalry.

Everyone in the company referred to him as 'Benny' and he "was well known and liked by Reno's men." He was assigned as Reno's adjutant and was a dear friend to Reno.

Reno and his men came under heavy Indian rifle fire at the crossing. Hodgson, in the process of fording the river, caught a bullet in the leg. The bullet traveled through his leg and entered his horse, immediately killing the animal. Hodgson's leg was shattered beyond repair.

"Fighting shock, he managed to grab a stirrup kicked out to him by another soldier. He was dragged through the water to the opposite shore."

Still fighting shock and struggling to overcome his shattered leg, he "managed to crawl part way up a steep bank before he was shot and killed by another Indian rifleman. His body rolled down the bank and came to rest near the water." There he lay until sometime later, after the battle had ended, and surviving soldiers buried the dead.

When he was found there was a look about him that frightened any who saw him. His eyes were filled with terror and horror. The body was buried in the same spot where it was found.

In the summer of 1983, a young and attractive native of Minnesota, Christine Hope, was a student intern at the battlefield. She came there for a partial rest and to complete some studies. Tours, talks and seminars occupied a part of her daily routine.

After a long day, she fell asleep on the sofa in her room. "Sometime after midnight she awakened for some reason and began to look around the room. It was pitch black, with only a shaft of moonlight coming in through a window across from the couch. She could see that the shaft of moonlight bathed a man's face.

"He appeared to be dressed in a form of contemporary [to 1876] clothing. He had a flowing handlebar mustache but what reached the deepest into her brain was his face, and the look in his eyes."

Chris commented later about what she saw.

"It was his eyes that got to me the most. It's hard to explain, but those eyes stood out. They were filled with incredible fright. They were filled with terror," she related to a friend. A few seconds later the ghost disappeared. She sat numbly in her position and couldn't move.

The following day, she and a friend, Tim Bernardis, walked near the river. They noticed a marker for one of the soldiers. Tim checked a guidebook that gave short biographies of those who died at the battlefield. He said the marker belonged to Second Lieutenant Ben H. Hodgson.

"Here is his picture," Tim said, showing her the young man's photo.

Chris' breath stopped.

"What's the matter?" Tim inquired.

Chris then told her story about the man she'd seen in her room about midnight. It was the ghost of Hodgson. There was no doubt about it as far as Chris was concerned.

The 'Mystery of Hoyle's Castle' took place in White Oaks, New Mexico Territory during the 1880's and is a mystery to this day.[8]

Andy Hoyle was a mine superintendent and a lonely man. Feeling that this loneliness was beyond endurance, he placed an ad in the lonely hearts section of an eastern newspaper, advertising for a mail-order bride. A young lady answered his ad and the two struck up a mail romance.[9]

Hoyle thought it most important that this young lady have a respectable place to live if she should decide to become his bride. During the written courtship he built a brick and stone mansion in the mining town of White Oaks. It had stained-glass windows, hand-carved pine and redwood paneling, and a lead pipe water system. It was decorated with the most expensive furniture of the period and was soon dubbed "Hoyle's Castle" by the area natives.

When he finished his monument to her, he wrote and proposed. She accepted. Sometime later, the young bride-to-be arrived by stage at White Oaks. Andy, like the gentleman he was, was present to meet her and carry her away to her new castle.

Hidden behind the castle walls, the couple conversed about the many things they felt and believed. During this time something went wrong. Neither Andy nor his bride-to-be enlightened the curious populace. Yet, something was wrong.

Shortly after she'd arrived, the young lady took her baggage, bought a ticket back home, boarded the next stage and was gone. She never returned.

Andy became a recluse and roamed the halls of his home at late hours of the night. He bemoaned the loss of his young lady and many said he started to drink heavily. One day, Andy Hoyle

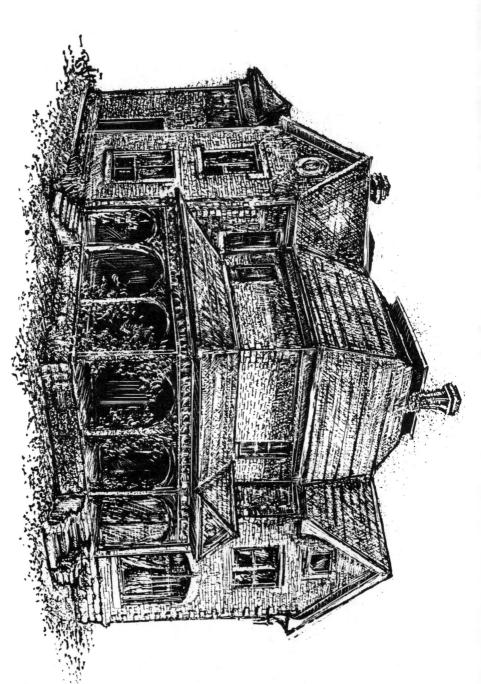

Hoyle's Castle

vanished. No one knew what happened to him. He just vacated the house, never to return.

The house still stands in the ghost town of White Oaks as a reminder of Andy and his bride-to-be. The truth of the mystery remains with the house. Why did she leave? Was he not the gentleman some thought him to be? What became of him? It is a mystery too difficult to solve at this day and time.

The last story is 'The Mystery of the Weeping Woman.' Exactly when it began no one knows. Some say it dates back to the Conquistadors in the 16th century.

It is the story of a beautiful young peasant girl whose natural beauty captured the hearts of all who saw her. She was unusually tall and had long, flowing black hair. Even the rich, young men of the day fell for her radiant beauty and would often seek her out and hope to win her favors.[10]

The legend relates that she had two young sons and, being a single parent, they were often a burden to her. They made it difficult for her to attend the many local fandangos. Craving the attention of the rich young men, La Llorona, as she was called, drowned her sons in the river.

Grief for her sons overcame her love of dances and she began to mourn their deaths. Day and night she walked the lonely river banks and moaned for their absence. It was too late. They were dead and would never come back to her. Her wailing became constant and the villagers often heard her cries. She grew thinner as she did not eat or sleep.

"Finally, when almost a skeleton, she died on the banks of the river. But her spirit could not rest. It was seen often by many, walking the banks of the river when darkness fell. Her wailing became a curse of the night." Today, her spirit appears at different times and in different areas of the Southwest.

"The legend of La Llorona has become part of Hispanic culture throughout the world. It is said she is everywhere now, and those who don't think of their children will see her and she will teach them a lesson."

Certainly, her story, like the others you will read within the pages of this book, becomes a part of the *Ghosts and Mysteries of the Old West*.

La Llorona Weeping For Her Children

A Town Born of Violence

In *Legends of the Spanish Southwest* by Cleve Hallenbeck, there is an account of a town born from violence. It deserves to be retold.[1]

"While generally known in the valley of the Rio Grande," Hallenbeck states, it is "little known elsewhere and never has appeared in print except in the form of a very brief synopsis."

The year was believed to be 1712 when a wagon train of colonists headed northward through El Paso. Their destination was the lovely northern region of the New Mexico territory. For three long, weary months the group moved their wagons foot by foot over the plateaus and mountain valleys of Zacatecas, Durango, and Chihuahua. At last, directly ahead of them, the *Jornada del Muerto* Desert spread itself − inviting them to pass if they dared.

So far they had encountered only friendly Indians. Since passing through Paso del Norte they had not even so much as seen these. Everyone joked openly about the warnings issued by the officials at Chihuahua and Carrizal. The travelers considered such warnings as nothing more than attempts to frighten newcomers; jokes played as a pastime by the bored, early frontier soldiers.

Nevertheless, unknown to the happy travelers, the wagon train wasn't alone. Every man, woman, child, wagon, rifle, and animal was stalked by the omnipresent eyes of Apache scouts. Moving with the silence of a snake's whisper, these scouts maintained advantageous positions along the trail while they scrutinized the passing wagon train; then they moved ahead to the next hiding place.

11

Born of Violence

The highly-skilled Apache surveillance quickly noticed the let-down of vigilance by members of the wagon train. On the third day out of El Paso, the Apache war party determined it was time to strike. The wagon train was now in a perfect position to be hit. They had camped on a spot surrounded by sand mounds and mesquite thickets. That night the Spaniards placed no guards on duty.

The Apaches hid their horses about a mile from the encampment. During the moon-less night, under the cover of the night's shadows, the relentless hunters of the desert moved silently to within a few feet of the sleeping, unsuspecting settlers. There they squatted and waited until dawn.

As the radiant New Mexico sun inched upward over the spiraling Organ Mountains, the camp was astir. Each person was excited and anxious to get underway. Fires from the previous night were refueled. Pots, kettles and pans were placed about the fires and soon the smell of coffee filled the air for miles around. The men, unaware of the peril which lay nearby, busied themselves with such meaningful duties and chores as reloading the wagons for the day's journey. Innocent children romped and played games, clamoring for free bits of food, while the women continued the drudgery of their daily routines; routines which were accepted in that day and time as part of a woman's world. No one had any idea of the hellish pain, suffering and death which hid within the surrounding clumps of salt-grass — waiting and watching, ready to pounce upon them without mercy or feelings of compassion. The unmistakable threat was there like a long, black, hovering cloud.

Although described as a savage by previous travelers, the Apache Indian was extremely intelligent regarding his way of life. So intelligent and cunning, as a matter of fact, that he could travel for miles without leaving a track or sign as to where he had just been.

Had but one of these pilgrims been skilled in the ways of the desert, he would have had people hidden behind their wagons at the first lifting of the sun above the horizon. He would have sent armed men on horseback into the surrounding area and flushed out the Apache. From this vigilance, the Apache would have fled.

The native animals knew. They had noticed the concealed Indians and knew they were stalking their prey — the settlers. The animals knew from experience that such a stalker was to be feared, watched, and most of all — avoided.

Born of Violence

All jack rabbits hid that morning. None hopped about in search of breakfast. The prairie dogs stayed in their burrows and refused to fill the morning air with their usual chirping. Even the common Finch was silent. No song exited from his throat that morning.

These were all signs an experienced trailblazer immediately noticed. But not these pilgrims. Instead, they sat about their campfires — laughing, talking, and stuffing their stomachs for the last time.

Perhaps it was a small child cresting a sand mound to conceal themselves while they passed waste, or perhaps a horse caught a whiff of a strange scent and became startled.

The joyous morning sounds were suddenly stilled as the shriek of an Apache carried upon the wind. A musket exploded. The swoosh of an arrow and then the melon-like sound it makes when it hits its mark was heard. Women began to scream. Men grabbed their muskets and fired in every direction without any sign of organization. Children ran haphazardly toward their mothers, praying for the safety they thought they would find. The fearless Apache warriors continued their assault upon the travelers with only one objective in mind — death to these travelers.

It was a complete surprise. And it worked. The wounded men, women, and children were mauled to death with clubs and knives. Their cries and pleas for mercy were drowned by the shrieking of the wild Apaches.

After they looted and fired the wagons, the Apaches herded away the horses and cattle. Within two hours after the start of the attack, the Apaches crossed the Rio Grande and headed west for their camp in the Mimbres Mountains — a place where pursuit was useless.

A lone rider, believed to be a Piros Indian, heard the noise of the attack. He hid himself where he could view what was happening. Knowing that he could be of no value at the scene, he remounted his horse and fled toward El Paso where he hoped he might alert help. He arrived in El Paso before noon. A mounted troop of soldiers left immediately.

Too late. At the massacre site they found the mutilated bodies of the men, women, and children of the wagon train. "The corpses of mothers still held, tightly clasped in their arms, the mutilated bodies of their children," Hallenbeck tells us. The mothers had "endeavored to the last to give them the protection that their children had confidently expected of them."

Born of Violence

Only one soldier spoke. He gave an order to dig the graves. There wasn't anything else anyone could say.

The next year, under Governor-General Mogollon's leadership, these same troops encountered the same Apaches. Only this time, it was the Apaches who had reason to remember what happened. Mogollon and his men slaughtered Apache men, women and children in revenge and retribution.

At the wagon train massacre site, later travelers stopped, said a prayer at the graves, and laid a stone around the garden. Many pulled weeds or cleared the area. Some even fixed new crosses over the graves. For nearly one hundred years this tradition continued. Finally, travelers stopped and stayed.

A little village started at this spot. At first it was called *La Aldea del Jardin de Las Cruces* (the little town of the garden of the crosses). More and more people settled in the valley. Several years later the name was shortened to Las Cruces.

As is usual with legends, there are many versions. Other versions have the massacred band composed of Catholic missionaries or Spanish soldiers. Regardless of who was buried in the mass grave by the Rio Grande, the site became a landmark for later travelers following the river north to Santa Fe.

Today, nearly three centuries later, Las Cruces, New Mexico, a town born out of violence, boasts many schools, churches, a library, a state university and nearly 60,000 residents. Though much has changed, one thing remains certain — born out of violence, its past continues to haunt it.

Terror of the Sacramento Mountains

The outlaw bandit John Morris, alias Morrison, was fifteen years old when he made his mark upon the annals of the Old West. Described as "evidently ambitious to outdo Billy the Kid and other notorious desperadoes," Morris lived up to his legend for three wild and woolly months in the New Mexico Territory. The citizens of Sacramento, La Luz, and Peñasco were constantly terrorized by him and his devilish deeds. Finally, in July 1886, he stood before the justice of that Old West.

On that same July day, an article appeared in the *Rio Grande Republican*, titled "Another Shooting Affray Near La Luz."[1] Two ranchers J.K. Ist and Dud Richardson, brought Morris to jail on that summer day. This is the true story of one they called the "boy bandit − the terror of the Sacramento Mountains," New Mexico Territory, 1886!

It had been two and a half months since the boy rode out on his own. He had been doing pretty well, too, he kept telling himself. Then, one day he unexpectedly met a rancher named Rochez. Rochez had a ranch in Dog Canyon in the northern section of Doña Ana County.

Morris saw his victim standing by a rock wall which was under construction. He looked around and saw no other person. All he needed to do was to shoot this man, steal what was needed, and flee the area.

He took the rifle out of the saddle shoulder.

"Yeah," he probably told himself as he checked to see there was a shell in the chamber. "This'll be easy."

He nestled down behind the stump of a tree and took careful aim.

Terror

Rochez had been sweating all morning because of the heat. Standing there, with his shirt off, he stooped to pick up one more rock. "This one," Rochez muttered, as he selected one made of sandstone. "I'll move it."

Behind him, he heard the rifle explode and felt the pain as the bullet tore its way into his body. Fortunately, he was able to run. He scampered toward the cabin. A second bullet found his arm as he gave a mad leap through the front door of his two-room cabin. There he waited!

Rochez spent the day in bed. Coiled in his right palm, like a rattler about to strike, was his .44 revolver.

About ten o'clock that night, Morris broke down the cabin door with his shoulder. He burst into the room and fired his sixgun. One bullet caught Rochez. Rochez's gun barked out hell's message. The projectile hit Morris. Morris turned and ran.

He made it to his horse and climbed aboard. The horse sensed it was time to go and headed out for new grazing ground. The boy bandit had escaped – this time.

Rochez recovered from his wounds. The "boy bandit" headed back to his old haunts in the Sacramento Mountains. During his flight, the horse gave out. Morris took his knife and cut the throat of the animal he had previously stolen from C. F. Hilton, an area rancher. In need of a mount, the horse thief returned to the Hilton ranch and stole a replacement.

The following morning, Tom Williams, the horse's owner, noticed his animal was missing. Word spread rapidly about the campfire. The men spread out and began to search for tracks. Richardson and Ist soon found Morris' trail. They conducted their own private manhunt for the boy bandit.

"Not over half a mile from the house of Dud Richardson," the *Rio Grande Republican* reporter wrote, the two cowboys came upon Morris' campfire. There the "daring young rascal had made his camp and staked out his horse. He surrendered without much trouble," the reporter concluded.

Ist and Richards bound the bandit in irons and brought him into town. He was "a mere boy, but is evidently of the most brutish and depraved nature. The bullet that Rochez fired at him struck him a little to the right of the nipple on his right breast, and, ranging around the rib, came out behind. The wound must have been very painful, but he rode all night after being shot. . . ."

16

Terror

Morris' exploits were recounted at the trial.

"His history of crime," the reporter added, "has something of a dime novel romance about it, as he's been an outcast."

Morris was found guilty of horse-thieving, attempted murder, petty stealing, several escapes from authorities, and terrorism.

"The only way to clip the wings of this rising young cut-throat," demanded the editor, "is to give him a good long term in the penitentiary."

And they did!

Robbery at Paso del Norte

This story took place on a winter Saturday, December 15, 1883. It is about Col. Albert J. Fountain of Mesilla, New Mexico and the time he was robbed and nearly murdered.[1]

What the sun does to the western New Mexico sky, after a day of radiant light, is unbelievable. Four or five clouds streak the sky as though drawn by some artist's pastel pencils. The setting sun colors them with pinks as soft as a baby's cheek. Majestic reds and purple grapes intermix with one another to form New Mexico's finest wines, both in the sky and the bottle.

It can be enough to mesmerize anyone into a form of neglect. Even neglect of one's own safety.

Col. Fountain admired the evening sky as he walked along a Juarez, Mexico street. It was more beautiful than ever, he thought. It was time to return to El Paso, Texas. But first, he'd stop and have a drink in a saloon. He'd been on business all day and one never knew who he might meet at one of the town hangouts.

Fountain walked in and stood at the bar, ordered his drink and pulled out a roll of greenbacks to pay. He removed a dollar with his right thumb and forefinger, laid it on the bar, and stuffed the roll back in his pocket.

Across the room, four Mexicans also admired the roll. One poked another with his elbow and nodded. The others smiled, revealing broken teeth as they nodded back.

The four left the saloon and walked up the street to wait in ambush for Fountain. Meanwhile, Fountain continued with his drink. He had not noticed the four men who'd eyed him so suspiciously.

18

Robbery

When he finished his drink, Fountain inquired if anyone in the saloon had heard of or seen the men whose names were listed on the extradition papers he carried, papers he'd obtained in Silver City. No one admitted knowing the men so Fountain turned to leave the saloon. He walked north from the plaza, aiming to catch a street car which would take him to El Paso.

As he stepped from the plaza, he noticed the four men who had watched him in the saloon. He walked toward them in an effort to get a closer look – believing they were possibly the ones he wanted. As he neared, they parted as if to let him pass between them. Then, the Mexicans surrounded him.

One of them drew a knife. He gave a wide sweep with the knife in an effort to murder Fountain. Snagging on the coat pocket, the knife caught hold and was deflected by the presence of the extradition papers.

At the same time, Fountain's right hand was moving back and up in search of his sixgun. He took a step back.

Suddenly, the thought flashed through his mind that he'd left his gun at the border crossing in El Paso. His military training permitted no flinching at this sudden turn of fate. Instead, he took two more steps backwards and again behaved as if to draw his sixgun.

His hand knew the gun was absent as it went in search of nothing, but the bluff worked. The four Mexicans turned and ran.

Without a handgun, the dignified Fountain set about readjusting his suit clothes. He noticed the coming street car and hurried to catch it.

It wasn't until he arrived in El Paso, however, that he reported the robbery to the law. The bandits had picked his pockets. A treasured watch with his monogram on the back, received while serving as Senator from Texas, was taken.[2] Also, he told the law officers, a roll of money and checks had been taken. The cash he valued at around $20 and the checks were said to be about $460.

Asked to describe the four men, Fountain's description fit a gang of outlaws who called themselves the 'Wolves.' They were known to have committed several robberies and even some murders along the rough U.S.-Mexico border area. No one, as yet, had been able to bring any of them to justice.

19

Robbery

A short time later, Col. Fountain arrived at his ranch in La Mesilla, New Mexico. Perhaps this incident was a foreshadowing of that which was to come. A warning, foretelling the cold day in February, 1896, when Fountain and his youngest son vanished somewhere in the mystical White Sands east of the Organ Mountains. Duty, however, would not allow such a man to heed any warnings.

Saturday Night Lynching

Don Evangelisto Chavez returned to his home in Las Cruces on May 4, 1883. He brought with him a picture which he showed to the editor of the *Rio Grande Republican*. The picture was taken in Lordsburg, New Mexico Territory.[1]

This is what he knew about the photo.

It began last Friday night when a cowhand named Welch and his partner were sleeping in adjoining beds in the same room.

Welch waited. Finally, around 1:30 a.m. Saturday morning, he climbed out of his bed, slipped on his boots, and reached for his revolver. The hand-grip felt cold in his palm.

He pointed the barrel toward the sleeping body of his partner. His finger laced itself across the trigger and every muscle tightened. The barrel held steady and then shattered the stillness with an explosion of fury. The projectile sped along its trajectory until it found its mark in the body of the unnamed partner.

The victim felt the searing heat as the bullet pierced him but all he did was grunt. It was fatal.

The editor inquired as to what Welch did next.

The murderer set out to throw the bed clothing about the room. He even picked up some of his own blankets and threw them on the floor. He wanted to make it look like the two men fought.

There was his partner's gun. He picked it up and fired one round into the wall in an effort to make it appear as though the partner had attacked him first. 'That should do the trick,' Welch probably told himself.

Saturday Night

The door opened. In walked several spectators to see what the shooting was about. Welch began to relate his story. They listened. Finally, despite their feelings, they did nothing at this time. One can visualize what must have happened.

They began to meet later that morning in the saloon. As they did, one of them talked more than the others about this Welch and what kind of guy he was. "After all," he must have hollered, "his partner was a man we all knew. He was always a quiet and inoffensive sort of chap. And this Welch hombre, everyone knew what sort of rawhide he was made of. He was always a notoriously bad character. . . ."

Upon this premise, the citizens of Lordsburg undertook the following mayhem on Welch.

Later that night they armed themselves with pistols, shotguns, and a couple of ropes. It was just like a Hollywood western. Visions of the intense and determined townspeople, as in the movie *Death of a Gunfighter*, come to mind. Angry men and women set out to lynch Welch before another New Mexico sun burst open in the east.

They pursued him until they caught him.

"Hold him tight," someone shouted.

Four men grabbed him. They held him as two others tied his hands behind his back. All the time he cursed them to hell for their vigilante actions.

After securing his hands behind his back, another man slipped the hangman's noose around the killer's neck and tightened it.

Raging shouts arose from the mob as they jeered Welch."

"Hang him! String him up!" the angry mob jeered.

"Let me pull the damn rope!" another probably shouted. He grabbed the rope and began to pull.

If Welch was able to relate his thoughts, they probably would be similar to these. He sensed the binding hemp shut off his air supply. "It didn't really hurt," he thought. It just cut off his breath. It became more like panic.

Within a matter of a few seconds, the grape hues of death filled Welch's face. His legs struggled to find something. What could that something be? "Wasn't there ground there just a moment ago," he might have reasoned.

Saturday Night

Cheers from the townspeople arose as Welch's legs finally ceased their fruitless search. The 'law-abiding' citizens of Lordsburg had set an example of what would happen to future killers who operated in their small town.

It wasn't until late Sunday, the next day, that they removed Welch's body from the hanging tree.

Earlier that same day, the Southern Pacific train passed through the town of Lordsburg. "The body attracted considerable attention among the passengers on the eastbound," wrote the reporter for the *Republican*.

This Lordsburg lynching was just one of the many instances of mystery, mayhem, and madness which occurred in Territorial New Mexico!

Ben Williams

Gunsmoke on Main Street

"New Mexico political history has no peer for intrigue, assassination, cabals, and general conniving," writes A. M. Gibson in *The Life and Death of Col. Albert Jennings Fountain*. "The focus of this turmoil was Doña Ana County."[1]

Col. Albert Jennings Fountain, the Republican czar of Doña Ana County since 1875, dominated the scene with his iron hand clutching the political throat of Southern New Mexico. However, Albert Bacon Fall, a Democrat from Texas, weakened that grip beginning with the day Fall set foot in the New Mexico Territory.

For nearly two decades, the two men fought bitterly for supremacy. Fountain described the struggle "as one perhaps to the death" in a letter to a friend in 1895.[2]

This story took place in 1893 during that political death struggle, and didn't explode until the night of Saturday, September 14, 1895. That was the night the citizens of Las Cruces smelled 'Gunsmoke on Main Street.'

Judge Albert B. Fall and his gang, composed of the infamous Oliver Lee, Fall's brother-in-law Joe Morgan, suspected cattle rustler Jim Gilliland, and the lusty young gunman Billy McNew, wholeheartedly approved the appointment of Ben Williams as United States Marshal. None of them voiced disapproval when Williams was also commissioned a Deputy Sheriff of Doña Ana County.

Yet, when they learned that Williams made no distinctions in those he arrested, they just as rapidly changed their minds. Williams was a man who didn't care what political brand a man wore if he was guilty, or suspected of being guilty, of a crime.

25

When he learned that Fall protected suspected criminals from prosecution, he set out to get him and other local office holders.

Judge Fall came to Las Cruces in 1887. He was born in Kentucky in 1861. Drifting west early in life, he settled in Texas for a while, and then moved on to New Mexico. He worked for several years in the Kingston, New Mexico diggings as a hard rock miner. This position helped him to develop all the noisy, blustering, uncouth qualities he possessed. Yet, despite this crudeness, he was compulsively ambitious. Forsaking his trade in the mines, he read a few law books (some would say obviously the wrong ones), and moved to Las Cruces where he set up his practice. In no time at all, he had rallied local Democrats and even established his own paper — the *Independent Democrat*. In 1892, he defeated Fountain by a landslide for the district's state legislative seat. The following year, President Grover Cleveland appointed him judge for the Third Judicial District.

Oliver Lee was Fall's rival only in one sense. Where Fall was establishing a political empire, Lee was establishing a range dynasty. Lee came to the New Mexico Territory in 1884 with his half-brother, Perry Altman. They left Taylor County, Texas in search of new range. Both decided to settle on the western slopes of the Sacramento Mountains in northeastern Doña Ana County. The following year, they moved their families and cattle to the new location — situated on the edge of Dog Canyon. Seeing the range had potential, Lee wrote to friends back in Texas, asking them to join them. Among those who came were Billy McNew and Jim Gilliland.

Legends flourished about the three men as they rode roughshod about the countryside. One told of a nameless grave near the Coe Ranch; the inscription being, "he called Oliver Lee a liar."[3]

"Everyone was afraid of him," Margaret Behringer wrote to A. M. Gibson. "He was a crack shot and never missed. He could shoot the eye out of a bird in the air and never miss. He was a fine looking man; always a gentleman — very quiet."[4]

In 1892, Fall appointed Lee, Gilliland, and McNew United States Deputy Marshals. In addition, all three had been appointed as Deputy Sheriffs by Guadalupe Ascarte — Fall's puppet-on-a-string sheriff.[5]

Gilliland was described as "never in town that he wasn't drunk, and he could get drunk the nastiest way of any man. He

26

Albert Bacon Fall

not only smelled bad — he was always doing something he shouldn't." It was also said that he and McNew "treed the town every time they rode in." He often roamed the streets of Las Cruces armed with sixguns and carrying a shotgun. He was a bully who harassed and intimidated innocent men, women, and children.[6]

Morgan, like Gilliland, was a bully who possessed one other outstanding quality — he was a braggart. Rumor had it that he'd left Texas with a posse on his trail for someone's murder. With his brother-in-law on the local bench, he meandered about Las Cruces enjoying the freedom of a mad dog.

Young Billy McNew was the pack brat. With Gilliland, he comprised the hard-core center of the gang. He also hailed from Texas and came to New Mexico about the same time as the others.

Being a good Democrat, Williams reported his findings about these three men to the party leaders, but to no avail. Instead, the party leaders quickly reprimanded Williams. Meeting behind closed doors, Fall, who controlled the other party leaders, tried Williams in secret, found him guilty of "not being a good Democrat," and quickly removed him from office.

At about the same time in 1894, Williams "through Fountain's influence, was appointed a brand inspector with the Southeastern New Mexico Stock Growers' Association." In addition, he was made a local constable of Precinct 20 in Las Cruces.

The Cattle Growers' Association was formed in March, 1894 when twenty-one representatives of the great and powerful corporation-managed cattle companies, "whose brands ranged over a territory greater in extent than some states or even some nations," met in Col. Fountain's office. Fountain acted as association attorney and drafted a constitution and bylaws for the new organization. The members met later that month in Lincoln, New Mexico Territory to ratify Fountain's work. W. C. McDonald, manager of the Carrizozo Land and Cattle Company, was elected president of the association.[7]

As brand inspector for the association, Williams was to watch the various herds in the area and catch any cattle rustlers who might be increasing their own herd by illegally branding cattle from another ranch. No one knows for sure who 'sicked' him on Lee, Gilliland, and McNew, but Williams went after them with a strong determination to succeed.

Gunsmoke

Oliver Lee

"My first bad break," he was later quoted as saying, "was to get after a gang of organized cattle thieves. Several of these criminals belonged to the gang of bogus Deputy United States Marshals," he added, referring to Fall's gang of followers.[8]

In November, 1894, Doña Ana County held an election. Ben Michelson served at the polls during the election. He later testified that Albert Fall showed up during the voting, "unlawfully entered the ropes surrounding the polling places," and told him "that if anyone created any disturbance [it was his job] to have them removed and arrested."[9]

Shortly before noon on that election day, Fall and Lee rode to the village of Doña Ana — a few miles north of Las Cruces. They discovered 84 ballots had been cast by the voters. The ballots, they learned, were about evenly divided between Democrats and Republicans.

While the election judges ate dinner at their respective homes, Fall and Lee switched the real boxes for stuffed ones filled with ballots marked unanimously Democratic.[10]

Williams also discovered this bit of treachery. In the *Rio Grande Republican* article quoted above, Williams stated Fall and Lee "were on hand to see that the stuffed ballot boxes were counted. I soon discovered that I'd committed another offense against these high toned Democrats," he added.

Williams also related how one of the Fall gang, probably Morgan, called him aside and told him there were fifteen assassins waiting for orders "from headquarters" to kill their assigned Republican leaders.

Williams, a loyal Democrat all his life, set out to gather evidence against these fifteen men. Word spread rapidly that he'd betrayed his party and he was now considered to be "a dangerous man and must be gotten rid of."

Doña Ana Sheriff Guadalupe Ascarte, the corrupt, vile tool of Albert Fall, received word to hire "a bad man from the Sacramento Mountains who was to carry out all instructions given him from headquarters."[11]

Meanwhile, Williams' investigation drew him closer to Judge Fall and his cronies. By the summer of 1895 he had in his possession several warrants for the arrest of nearly all fifteen men.

An unnamed Mexican deputy was sent to another town. There he swore out a complaint against Williams. The charge

Billy McNew

Jim Gilliland

was that Williams had violated Section 10 of an act passed in 1887 governing the conditions whereby a lawman might carry firearms within the city limits of a town.

The warrant was issued for Williams, given to the Sacramento badman to serve, and Williams was arrested in early August, 1895. He was placed in iron shackles, man-handled into a nearby wagon, and hauled off to Mesilla, New Mexico Territory, "even though there were two Justices of the Peace in Las Cruces."

In the interview Williams gave to the *Republican* editor, he also said he was arraigned before the Justice of the Peace "who enjoys the reputation of being the most stupid in the county."

Williams presented his case with mastery and skill. He was quick to point out that he was a city constable, and that, despite the New Mexico law against carrying weapons in town, he was allowed to carry a pistol in the performance of his duty. He called attention to the fact that Oliver Lee "habitually" carried firearms and was "in constant violation of the same law" but nothing had been done to him. He presented evidence showing that when he was arrested he had "in his possession for service warrants for cattle thieves."

Despite all this, the 'sapient' justice, acting under orders "from headquarters," found Williams guilty. He was sentenced and had to post a bond of $500.

On Sunday, August 11, Williams was approached again by the same man who'd arrested him just a few days earlier. "Without a warrant or complaint, [this man] arrested him again for carrying weapons."[12]

Quickly hauled off to jail, he demanded a hearing. Deputy Sheriff Oliver Lee told him that charges would be brought against him the following day and he'd be delivered up to the justice of the peace at that time. Finally, after much arguing and bickering, Williams was released after posting yet another bond.

A change of venue was in order and, at the insistence of Albert Fall, the new trial was transferred to La Luz — a distance of one hundred miles away in the Sacramento Mountains.

It was all too obvious by now that Oliver Lee and his badge-carrying bandits were out to "get the pot-bellied Ben Williams."

Oliver Lee struck again on Friday, August 16, 1895, when he approached Williams and arrested him for carrying a weapon within the city limits of Las Cruces.

"Mr. Williams, at the time of his arrest," stated the *Rio Grande Republican*,[13] "had a pistol, and the deputy sheriff making the arrest had prominently displayed upon his person two pistols which he openly and habitually carries."

The arrest, the article also pointed out, was made without any complaint being filed or without the issuance of any legal warrant of arrest. Williams once more was carted off to the local county jail and placed under the custody of Sheriff Ascarte.

Called upon to defend himself, Williams immediately demanded that he be placed on trial. Ascarte informed Williams that he wasn't certain which Justice of the Peace was to handle the case, "as he had not yet been advised."

Williams then demanded when he could have a trial.

"I don't know," Ascarte snapped.

Williams told Ascarte he'd post a bond of any amount up to $5,000. Ascarte ignored him.

Finally, by four o'clock that afternoon, Williams was brought before Mr. Valdez and a complaint made as to why he'd once more been unjustly arrested.

An unnamed witness testified that at the time of the arrest, Williams carried a pistol. Williams admitted such was the case and once more undertook to explain that at the time he was in the performance of his duty. He informed them he was, after all, a constable of Precinct Number 20 in Las Cruces, that he had in his possession certain warrants which he was in the process of issuing, and that these warrants were for the charges of cattle thieves.

No one contradicted his word.

After much arguing on both sides, they reached a decision.

"Evidence conclusively established the fact that, at the time of his arrest, Ben Williams was a constable of Precinct Number 20 and that he was in the legal discharge of his duties of that office." The charges were dropped and Williams left the courtroom a free man – at least for the moment.

Oliver Lee, a "tall, lithe man with small hands and feet and wide-spaced eyes" then presented a bill for his expenses. His bill for services rendered amounted to $25. Adding the expenses for the others involved, the total cost to the citizens of Doña Ana County came to over $100.

Despite his acquittal, the harassment of Ben Williams continued. Albert Fall made it clear to Oliver Lee that Williams was not to succeed.[14] With the aid of Joe Morgan, who'd recently returned from Texas where he'd been extradited for murder by none other than Ben Williams, Lee and his henchmen dogged Williams' every step. Likewise, Williams, still choosing to remain totally loyal to Col. Fountain, never gave up his search for the cattle thieves named in his warrants. The battle of wills grew hotter.

Mrs. Williams, Ben's wife, became ill during the early days of September, 1895, and was confined to her bed. With this weighing upon his mind, Constable Williams made his rounds a bit early on that Saturday evening of September 14th. By 9:45 p.m. he'd concluded those rounds and was "quietly heading home."

His spurs jangled as he strolled down the east side of Las Cruces' Main Street. The night was still and the stars shone like glimmering candle lights in the cloudless sky. Nearly everyone was at home now, Williams felt.

Everyone, that is, but Albert Fall, Joe Morgan, and two other men. Instead, Fall, Morgan and a third man stood, waiting silently in the dark shadows just around the corner of Dresseur's building. The fourth man hid somewhere atop a nearby building.

As Williams stepped in front of Dresseur's building, Fall, Morgan and the third man stepped out from the demonic shadows. Morgan raised his sixgun and aimed it directly into Williams' face, a distance of about one foot.

There was a moment of time, which to Williams must have seemed an eternity, when his mind went completely blank. All thoughts of his wife were erased from his mind. He heard the sound of the hammer as it clicked backwards and came into firing position.

The images of the three men began to attach themselves to names as he quickly recognized the man behind the cocked sixgun as Joe Morgan. Williams' left hand began an upward sweeping motion in an attempt to deflect the route of the approaching bullet. His head involuntarily jerked to one side just as the pistol exploded with hell's fury.

The bullet grazed his temple and continued down the street before striking a building. The closeness of the blast, however, delivered severe powder burns to Williams' face.

As rapidly as Williams' left hand had begun moving, so also his right hand undertook that habitual movement of slapping leather. It came up holding his own sixgun. His finger tightened around the trigger and squeezed without any thought to his action. He fired a second time.

Unlike the first bullet, the second found its mark and hit Morgan in the arm. Morgan stumbled back a step from the blast.

Meanwhile, Fall moved to get behind Williams. Suddenly, Williams felt his hat fly from his head as Fall's bullet pierced it.

Williams turned and jerked off another shot in the direction of Albert Fall. He missed. At the same time, Morgan managed to fire another shot. A burning sensation entered Ben's left arm and he felt the bullet traveling in slow motion through his arm at the elbow, journeying upwards, and exiting out from his shoulder. He fell to the ground.

He fired two more shots at Morgan. Fall and Morgan ducked to avoid being hit as, by now, Williams was shooting at anything that moved. Williams staggered back to his feet and ran to the west side of the street in an attempt to seek cover for himself.

Just as his body slammed itself against a nearby building, two more shots struck nearby. From atop the building, the waiting fourth man fired these last two shots.

Almost as soon as it started, it stopped. The townspeople heard shots and ran to see what was happening. This, no doubt, contributed to ending the gunfight.

The man on the building roof escaped. The third man standing in the shadows with Fall and Morgan ran down the alley and no one found him. Of course, Fall and Morgan weren't going to identify him.

Fall and Morgan were arrested that same night, posted bond, and were released to appear before the investigating Grand Jury.

Friends surrounded Ben Williams and removed him to Mr. Sturrey's rooms next to Riley's shop.

Lying in her bed, within the safety of her home, Mrs. Williams heard the shooting. In spite of her weakened condition, she jumped from her bed and ran towards the door.

"They've shot Ben," she screamed as her mother attempted to coax her back down upon the bed. Tears filled her eyes and she paid no attention to her mother's efforts.

"We want the doctor, for Ben Williams is shot!" she heard one man exclaim.

"Dr. Mickey and Dr. Lane were at once summoned and proceeded to dress the wounds," the reporter informed his readers.[15] The following morning, Williams was moved to his own home and bed. He recovered from his wounds, but not before he and Col. Fountain were brought before a Grand Jury in Doña Ana County.[16]

Ben Williams moved to El Paso, Texas shortly after this shooting incident. He never gave up his pursuit to lay a charge of cattle rustling or brand changing on Oliver Lee. Williams continued to believe he would some day bring Lee to court in Texas or New Mexico. Many years later, Williams and Fall became friends and even had business dealings.[17]

Col. Fountain, on the other hand, disappeared under strange circumstances four months later after he and Williams had acquired the evidence they thought would convict Lee, Gilliland, and McNew.

Fall, Joe Morgan, and the other two ambushers never came to trial for their actions during the night Las Cruces citizens smelled gunsmoke on Main Street.

Old Buck's Ghost Still Roams New Mexico

Here is a humorous, intriguing, and supposedly true tale. Frank Benton tells this story about New Mexico Senator Stephen W. Dorsey. It took place in northern New Mexico and the time period is not known.[1]

A certain Englishman was interested in buying cattle from Senator Dorsey. Being a careful man, the Englishman refused to take Dorsey's figures regarding the number of cattle Dorsey had on hand and insisted on personally counting them.

"Jack," Dorsey told his ranch foreman, "I want you to find me a small mountain around which a herd of cattle can be circled several times in one day. This mountain must have a kind of natural stand where men can get a good count of the cattle stringing by, but where they can't possibly get a view of what is going on outside."

Having ridden Dorsey's range for a considerable number of years, the foreman had no trouble in locating just the perfect mountain. They stationed the Englishman and his bookkeepers on the mountain's side where the canyon opened. There he could make his tallies.

Jack Hill and the other range hands separated the cattle into two groups — each containing about 500 head. They kept the groups about a mile apart. When everyone was positioned and ready, the cowboys drove the first group into the canyon to be counted. This group was hardly out of sight before the second group entered.

While the second group entered the canyon, the cowboys rapidly drove the first herd around to the other side of the mountain. When the second group arrived, the counting began again.

Old Buck

This went on all morning. The cowboys drove in one group just as the other group left, and the Englishman kept on counting. About noon, the men all decided to take a break. During the break, Dorsey's foreman told the Englishman the cowboys were still holding the bulk of the herd back in the hills, waiting to be counted.

Three hours later, the cattle were hungry, thirsty, and footsore. It was estimated each steer had traveled about thirty miles that day just circling the mountain. Several began to drop by the wayside and lie down. One steer was a bobtailed, lophorned, old yellow steer with a game leg.

"There is more bloody, blasted, lophorned, bobtailed, yellow, crippled brutes than anything else, it seems," the Englishman spoke up at one point, having noticed the same steer during its numerous trips around the mountain.

Dorsey, worried that the Englishman would soon discover his trick, called Jack aside. He told Jack to be sure and cut that steer out of the herd on the next time around.

Jack cut him out and ran the steer off several yards. But the old yellow bull, known to the ranch hands as 'Buck', just limped back down into the canyon and rejoined the herd.

Again, Dorsey called Jack aside and told him to *get rid of that steer*. This time they ran the bull off further. About half an hour later, here came Buck, meandering back into the canyon.

Dorsey then told the Englishman there was only one more herd to count and signaled Jack to ride around and stop the endless circle.

Once more having run Buck off, the last herd was brought by. Sure enough, there was old Buck staggering along with the rest.

That night, several of the ranch hands heard Senator Dorsey groaning in his sleep. One of them awoke the Senator to see what was the matter. Dorsey told them he'd been having a nightmare about that blasted bull – Buck.

The Senator insisted they ride out to the canyon and see about the bull. Sure enough, there in the New Mexican moonlight, old Buck was still staggering around and around the mountain.

It was nearly a week later when they again heard about Buck. One of the cowboys, riding by that area of the ranch, noticed the big bull lying dead along the well-worn path he'd traveled so many times.

Old Buck

"No one ever rides that way on moonlight nights now," Frank Benton tells us in his tale. "The cowboys have a tradition that during each full moon old Buck's ghost still limps down the canyon."

Col. Fountain and the Twice Hung Man

For God's sake!" screamed a woman. "The dead has come to life!"

Her shrill voice brought back the crowds' attention to what had just happened. The body of William Wilson, who had been tried, convicted, and executed for murder, was still breathing.

These events led to that fateful moment in Old West history. A moment when angry New Mexicans took a man who had paid for his crime, and with beastly fury, rehung him from the same gallows. It's authentic, old-west justice — 1875 style.[1]

Wilson seemed to "just drop in at the Robert Casey place." He was looking for a grubstake.[2] Casey, desperate for help, hired him on the spot. As the days passed, Wilson appeared to be a good worker.

The Casey family also owned another farm, the Feliz place. Sometime after Wilson began working on the Casey farm; he, Casey, and several other workers went to the Feliz place to build a stock house and corral.

After the work was completed, Casey ordered Wilson to hitch up the ox wagon and take it back to the main farm. Robert Casey and the others remained behind to care for a few unfinished chores. Wilson complied.

Several days later, the four Mes brothers crept into the Feliz camp and stole their horses. This left Casey and his men afoot. The journey back would be a long walk.

Meanwhile, Wilson had made friends with a man named Harper who worked at another ranch. Harper, it seems, was working and biding his time until he could go to California.

40

Twice Hung Man

Robert Casey

The prospect of going to California excited Wilson. He came by the next day and told Mrs. Casey that he'd like his wages so he could go also. She gently informed him he'd have to wait for her husband to return from Feliz. Wilson seemed content to wait.

He spent his time cleaning and fixing his traps in preparation for the journey. He spoke freely with the Casey children — especially young Lily.

He boasted about his past life of criminal activity. Why, he'd even spent time, he bragged, in Sing Sing Prison. He was, in the vernacular of 1875, "wild and woolly and hard to curry."

The following morning Casey arrived home around two. His wife told him about Wilson's request.

"All right. Tell the clerk in the store to settle with Wilson and pay him all that's coming to him. Have him do this first thing in the morning."

The sky cleared into the yellow hue of a New Mexico sunrise. Wilson entered the Casey kitchen. Quickly, he gathered kindling. His body shivered across the floor to the stove and he lit the blaze with the match in his right hand. The fiery warmth from the inferno limbered his joints and his knuckles popped as he stretched.

"All the time," writes Lily Casey Klasner "he talked volubly about how anxious he was to do all he could before leaving us and he was very expressive of his appreciation of all that we'd done for him while he stayed with us."[3]

Wilson left the Casey house but returned within a matter of minutes. He wanted to know if he could tell Mr. Casey good-bye in person. After all, he now had his grubstake. Mrs. Casey informed him that her husband was asleep.

"Mrs. Casey, I wouldn't have you wake him up for anything in the world," Wilson responded.

Wilson returned to his horse and rode off toward Lincoln, New Mexico. He spent the next two weeks listening to the honky-tonk sounds of the saloons before looking for Harper. Harper, on the other hand, had secured his grubstake and headed for California without telling Wilson. Wilson was devastated when he learned this.

Casey, back at his farm, was persuaded by friends to stand with Col. Mickey Cronin in the upcoming political convention; a convention scheduled to begin on August 2, 1875.

Casey finally agreed.

Twice Hung Man

The convention met on time. A gang of desperados, headed by Major Lawrence G. Murphy, was angry because they had been cheated out of representation at the convention. Around noon the convention took a break. Mr. Casey asked Edmund Welch to join him for dinner at the Wortley Hotel. Welch agreed and the two men walked toward the hotel.

They met Wilson on their way to the hotel. Casey invited him to come along and he accepted. The men enjoyed their meal. Casey paid the bill and Wilson departed from the company of his host. Welch remained with Casey and the two talked freely of the day's activities.

Murphy and his henchman, Jimmie Dolan, stopped Wilson as he walked away from Casey. They ushered him into one of the stores. The two offered Wilson $500 if he would gun down Casey. They further guaranteed that they would take care of any legalities. Wilson was even assured that they had people in high places who would influence the Governor.

Wilson fell for their lie. He accepted the gun and ammunition they offered him. Now he only had to kill his former employer.

He watched for Casey and then hid himself behind a nearby house. When Casey was within fifteen feet, Wilson fired his rifle. The bullet hit the target in the hip.

Casey staggered but didn't fall. He moved toward the cover of an adjoining house. Wilson pursued and the two met behind the house. Wilson fired his rifle a second time before Casey could get off a shot. The bullet fiercely ripped its jagged path through Casey's mouth, leaving massive damage and bloody pulp where teeth had once been.

Mrs. Casey was summoned and came. Her husband died as she stood nearby the following day. He never said anything about his murderer.

Wilson's trial convened in October, 1875. Rumors spread that Murphy's rogues would cause a jail break before or after the trial.

"Mrs. Casey," Captain Fechet advised, "if I were you, I would not believe a single one of that crowd of dirty scoundrels. Don't trust them at all, for they'll do anything on God's earth to turn Wilson free."

"My God!" the bereaved widow replied. "I want the law to take its course. I'm sure he'll get full justice and I want that above all else for the sake of my children."

Twice Hung Man

"You're exactly right, Mrs. Casey," Fechet staunchly assured her. "We'll bring the murderer to justice. I left him in charge of my sergeant and eight men, and gave them orders to shoot the first man who tried to approach the prisoner.

"You need not be uneasy about a mob's taking him away from me. If they do so, they'll have to kill me and my nine soldiers as well. We intend to see him convicted and hung! I'm sure Major Clendenin will support me in this statement to the extent of using every soldier in Fort Stanton!"

With that he left.

Wilson replied "not guilty" when questioned about his plea. Immediately, his attorneys, Simon B. Newcomb and William L. Rynerson from Mesilla, requested the court to grant a continuance. Two material witnesses were absent and couldn't be found.

"Objection!" screamed Col. A.J. Fountain, also from Mesilla, who was serving as prosecutor.

"Sustained," Judge Warren Bristol declared.

The selection of the jury and the trial took four days and wasn't without excitement. On the third day, Captain Fechet, who personally guarded Wilson, discovered some alarming action.

The prisoner had his hands down between his knees and there was "a slight movement of his shoulders." Fechet drew his revolver. He held it to Wilson's head. No one moved.

"Wilson, what are you trying to do?" Fechet demanded. "If you make another move you're a dead man!" The Captain moved slowly to a position where he could view Wilson's hands. It was obvious the prisoner was about to free himself. Fechet became furious with the people and began to shout.

"Whose work is this, I'd like to know? Mr. Sheriff, get your key and tighten those handcuffs up good and tight on the prisoner; also do the same for his leg shackles."

On the fourth day the jury was charged to return a verdict. It took them 15 minutes. The verdict was guilty.

Wilson was sentenced to hang on November 11, 1875. His attorneys tried to secure a new trial. No such luck!

Murphy's men persuaded Governor Samuel B. Axtell to grant a reprieve until December 18th. This would allow the governor more time to consider the facts.

Col. Fountain immediately set out to speak with the Governor. In his militaristic manner, Fountain informed the Governor of the facts as he knew them to be. Axtell, who believed Murphy's story of a gunfight in the street to be accurate, now chose to believe Fountain's story.

On the day of the hanging, Wilson was escorted by three companies of soldiers as he moved toward the noose. Major Clendenin was determined that no prisoner would escape from him. As for Captain Fechet, he continued his "personal pledge to Mrs. Casey" in guarding the prisoner himself. One could see he was taking great pride in escorting Wilson to the thirteen steps of the gallows.

When Wilson reached the top of the gallows, whom should he meet but his fellow conspirator – Major Murphy.

"Major, you know you are the cause of this. You promised to save me, but...." These were the last words Wilson uttered. Murphy wasted no time in kicking the trigger that sprung the trap door. It fell open. Wilson's body plunged endlessly into the scaffold's abyss. His legs scrambled for the platform that wasn't there. An explosion must have gone off somewhere inside his frying brain. 'Was this death?' he might have thought, as he continued forming soundless words to Murphy.

Murphy had his men take the body down and place it in a nearby coffin, which he'd supplied earlier. When they did, no one bothered to nail down the coffin lid. No one seemed to be paying any more attention. No one seemed to be in any hurry now that the excitement was over.

No one, except one curious Mexican lady.

She needed "just one more peak." No one would be the least resentful if she just lifted the loose lid and took a look at the corpse.

"For God's sake!" she screamed.

Those who'd turned away now turned back. Several of the townspeople began jeering Murphy and claimed this had been a trick to free Wilson. Murphy, on the other hand, held out that once a man had been punished for his crime, the law says you can't hang him twice.

"Ready!" commanded Capt. Fechet. He didn't have to continue his command. Murphy rescinded his opinion.

"I'm here to see the law carried out. I propose to keep the peace and allow no mob violence," Fechet concluded.

Twice Hung Man

Even while he spoke, friends of the murdered Mr. Casey grabbed a rope. One of them slipped the noose over Wilson's rope-burned neck while he lay in the coffin. He threw the other end over a scaffold beam.

Four men yanked Wilson from the coffin's walls. Five others took hold of the rope and pulled and pulled and pulled. Wilson's body again silhouetted the New Mexico sky where air rules and gravity can bring death. No man released the prisoner this time until they knew he was dead.

"The murder of Robert Casey," writes his daughter in her autobiography, "was avenged in what was the first legal hanging in Lincoln County, and what was also one of the more gruesome executions which might be termed a twice-told tale."

That was justice in the Old West in the year 1875!

The Black Coat Murder Mystery

We were traveling with the intention of killing anybody we could kill," Maximo Apodaca told his listeners. His head hung shamefully and his fingers nervously fiddled a tattered, brown cowboy hat.

Apodaca related the details of how he and Ruperto Lara had unmercifully slaughtered a family of three – the George Nesmith family of Three Rivers, New Mexico Territory. The damnable deed was committed in mid-August, 1882.

Maximo Apodaca was about "39 years old, with a receding forehead, and bad eyes." His blood-thirsty cohort was a Pueblo Indian with a manner described as "cool and indifferent."

Early on the morning of August 10, 1882, George Nesmith, his wife, and their 10 year-old adopted daughter climbed into their wagon. They were headed to Las Cruces. They had no idea they were to become the senseless victims of one of the bloodiest massacres in New Mexico's history.

At the same time, Apodaca and Lara traveled across the country "for the purpose of stealing."

This is the true account of their rendezvous with time, as told through the eyes of Maximo Apodaca – confessed child killer.[1]

The comprades left Apodaca's home in Santa Barbara, New Mexico, in July of that year and traveled to Rincon. From there they rode to San Diego, San Nicolas, and on to Tularosa. Apodaca camped at the outskirts of town while Lara rode in for supplies.

Upon his return to camp, the two became engaged in a bitter argument about Lara's tardiness in returning. Finally,

Lara told Apodaca he'd been at the home of a man named Rios. That ended the argument.

The following day, the two savage-minded men left for White Oaks. This was in late July, 1882. There they remained for nearly eight days.

At that time, White Oaks boasted two newspapers, three churches, a $10,000 brick school house, over 800 permanent citizens, and the famous Pioneer Saloon.[2]
The two spent some time there swaggering in and out of the saloon — a saloon which boasted that "it took a brave man and a cast iron stomach to partake of its pleasures."

Finally, traveling southwest, the two cut-throats stopped at the Carrizozo Ranch. After spending time visiting some women, they then rode out towards Three Rivers to see a man named Pomposo.

It was here, according to Apodaca, that Lara proposed they murder someone and rob them. They agreed to use hand signals to launch their attack upon the unsuspecting victims.

The following day they rode back to Tularosa where they remained for about three days at Rios' home. Then they rode off.

While on the trail, they met a wagon, which according to Apodaca, had "a crazy man tied inside." They passed it and continued on the trail.

A short time later, Apodaca and Lara arrived at White Water. After their arrival, the wagon with George Nesmith and his family reached White Water.

George Nesmith was a stout man, large in stature, about middle-aged, and wore a short beard. Mrs. Nesmith was a small, thin woman with red hair. No physical description exists for the little girl.

Several articles of clothing, food, and such were in the back of the Nesmith wagon. Among these were some red blankets, white blankets, and a black coat.

The time was around eleven o'clock in the morning.

Lara was the first to notice the Nesmith family and their wagon load of supplies. He motioned to Apodaca and the two men admired the family as the Nesmith family pulled into the resting spot.

After the wagon stopped, Lara and Apodaca went over to where Mrs. Nesmith was preparing the family's lunch. She asked the two men to sit and enjoy a bite with her family. They accepted.

Being that Apodaca was afoot, the Nesmiths invited him to ride on their wagon. Lara was riding a horse obtained from the Rios farm. Maximo climbed aboard the wagon and took the reins, after offering to drive in return for the ride. They traveled for some miles before stopping around 3:30 p.m. Afterwards, Apodaca again offered his services to drive the team of horses in exchange for not having to walk or ride double with Lara. After all, everyone agreed, they were all traveling in the same direction.

About two and a half hours later, the crimson sun began to sink into obscurity. Apodaca glanced back and to his left. Lara issued the hand signal to attack.

Apodaca reined in the horses. Instantly, there was an explosion behind him and the horses gave a slight bolt. Maximo turned to look back into the wagon.

"Jesus Christ!" Nesmith hollered.

Mrs. Nesmith lay crumpled across his lap. Blood, like the ever-flowing Rio Grande, was gushing from her mouth. Smoke escaped from the barrel of Lara's .44 pistol.

He fired again. The shot missed. A third shot volcanically exploded.

That bullet toppled George Nesmith backwards.

Apodaca grabbed at the rifle near him. He pointed it at the innocent girl who stood screaming beside her mother. Without a thought to his action, Apodaca fired. The young girl's slender body wilted like a morning glory in the mid-afternoon New Mexico sun.

She now lay at her mother's feet – dead!

Twenty-seven days later, on Wednesday, September 6, 1882, ranch hands Tom O'Connor and Sam Barlin cut across the unfrequented country between St. Nicholas Spring and the Jarillas. This area lies about half-way between San Augustine and White Water.

Off in the distance they saw an abandoned wagon. The two men turned their horses in that direction, and upon a closer inspection, they could see several buzzards and a couple of wolves standing by.

Black Coat

O'Connor drew his revolver, fired into the air, and the beasts fled. The two men proceeded to the wagon and dismounted.

Soon they saw the dried blood which had oozed from the wagon and spread itself over the axles and wheels and collected in pools upon the ground. More so, they had located the source of the nauseating stench that permeated the countryside for nearly a mile.

Barlin inspected the inside of the wagon. When he turned back the blankets from the bodies, he felt his own stomach turn upside down and he quickly turned his eyes away.

The three bodies were puffed beyond recognition due to the hot desert sun which daily boiled them into decomposition. O'Connor and Barlin quickly mounted their horses and rode off to San Augustine — the nearest town, about eighteen miles to the southwest.

"Nothing that we read of in fiction can excel in horror and mystery the murder which we published in our last issue. Even Edgar Poe's noted tale of *The Murder in Rue Morgue* lags in interest by the side of this later story of blood, and all the acuteness of his French detectives will be required in its unraveling."[3]

The newspaper continued to give, in great detail, all that pertained to the atrocious act. Because of the degree of decomposition, doubt was raised to the identify of the family. Belongings owned by George Nesmith and his family were found in the wagon but many felt it wasn't him.

"The inference would have been clear that the whole party had been murdered either out of revenge or to attain some private end. Robbery," the editor wrote, "was out of the question!"

He concluded that Indians were certainly not to blame as they would not have taken the time to cover the bodies.

Rumors spread as to the whereabouts of George Nesmith. The dead man's body was claimed to be that of Nesmith's partner or assistant — Mr. Gray.

On Saturday, March 10, 1883, the *Rio Grande Republican* stated that Mr. Gray had been in town the previous Thursday. Mr. Gray informed the press he'd come for the bodies of the family. He would transport them to the family plot near Blazer's Mill. It seemed another Nesmith child was buried there.

Black Coat

Before the burial, Gray claimed he'd removed parts of the dead man's body as proof of his word. One of these bodily parts was Nesmith's right arm. Everyone in the Three Rivers area remembered George Nesmith breaking his right arm. The fracture on the right arm, which Mr. Gray now had in his possession, clearly proved the dead body to be Mr. Nesmith.

The authorities now had one less question. The only remaining question – why were they murdered?

Reward posters for information leading to the arrest and conviction of the person or persons murdering the Nesmith family were issued. The Governor reportedly put up a large sum and by October 9, 1882, the civilian reward was almost $600.

Two and a half years later, in the March 21, 1885 issue of that same newspaper, the headlines read "MURDER WILL OUT!"

Excitement spread like March's winds upon the southern New Mexico desert concerning "the arrest and confession of the perpetrators of the triple murder." The story was repeated "from mouth to mouth and the public was curious to learn if the mystery was about to unfold."

It did!

Bounty hunter, James Lloyd, received "full credit of unraveling the mystery." He'd traced Apodaca and Lara through the black coat. The coat, which had recently come into Lloyd's possession, had been the personal property of George Nesmith. Further still, it was in Nesmith's possession at the time of his murder.

With this knowledge, Lloyd used his own method of detection. He discovered the coat was purchased by a man who lived at Santa Barbara – Mr. Felipe Telles. Telles' son-in-law, Ruperto Lara, and a friend, Maximo Apodaca, were both said to have been in the area at the time of the murder, Lloyd discovered. Lara, Lloyd learned, was in Mexico, across the border from El Paso.

The cowboy sleuth devised a cunning trap for Lara. He posed as a man looking for a partner to steal some cattle. Word went out among the rustler camps and into Mexico. Lara, like today's job seekers, answered the verbal ad.

By the Saturday preceding March 21, 1885, Lara was under arrest. Apodaca and Telles were also arrested. The latter two were brought before a Grand Jury the Tuesday preceding

March 21st. Apodaca made a full confession. His trial was scheduled for later that month.

A few days later Lara came to trial. The attorneys for the defense were Messers. Beer and Welch. Lara, the newspaper said, was unable to afford his own lawyers.

New Mexico was represented by "an array of legal talent seldom seen on one side of a criminal case in this territory." District Attorney Wade, Col. Albert J. Fountain of Mesilla, Judge Simon Newcomb and Col. William Rynerson served for the prosecution.

Apodaca turned state's evidence and was a prosecution witness. He testified to all he and Lara had done before and during the murder.

"I killed that child," he cried out. "I was so scared. Lara jumped inside and I was also in the wagon. I put my hands in the pocket of the man but I couldn't find anything.

"We then took the wagon off towards the left; a mile more or less. As soon as we got there, we took the trunk out of the wagon and broke it open and took several articles out of it. Lara took the black coat. . . ."

He went on to describe how many articles they stole. Afterwards, the two placed the bodies in a neater position and covered them with blankets. It was almost as though it was some afterthought, some Christian-like act within this Satanic deed.

They unhitched the horses and rode off towards San Diego crossing. There they spent the night. The following night, they slept at Santa Barbara, New Mexico. Next they went to Apodaca's house, and within a few minutes, moved on to Lara's house.

The outlaws visited with Lara's father, mother, and sister. After a good home-cooked meal, some strong coffee, and family conversation, Lara suggested he and Apodaca ride to El Paso. They did. Apodaca testified he spent the following four months in El Paso. Lara, on the other hand, had gone back to White Oaks for his family.

"Is this the black coat you referred to in your testimony, Mr. Apodaca?"

"This is the black coat that belonged to the man that was killed," Apodaca confessed, never once raising his eyes above the level of the coat or looking toward the jury. "Lara took it and kept it. He gave it to his father."

Black Coat

Lloyd testified he'd found the coat in the possession of Mr. Telles.

Telles, on the other hand, stated he'd received the coat from Lara's father in September, 1882 − a few days after the murder.

Mrs. Tucker, the next witness for the Territory, testified she had made the coat for Mr. Nesmith. A number of other witnesses linked Lara and Apodaca and placed them in the area of the murder.

Closing arguments were heard and Judge Wilson, presiding over the case, charged the jury on the law. The jury of eleven Mexicans and one American now retired to the jury room.

In less than five minutes, "it was announced they had agreed upon their verdict."

One by one the twelve members marched out. Each assumed his previous seat. The clerk's voice broke the painful silence.

"Gentlemen of the jury, have you agreed upon a verdict?" Clerk Bowman inquired.

"We have!"

"Jury stand up. Prisoner stand up."

Lara stood. His lips twitched.

"Jury, look upon the prisoner. What say you who are sworn, is the prisoner at the bar guilty or not guilty?"

An eternal pause filled the air.

The jury foreman opened his mouth. Nothing seemed to block the clear crackle of his words.

"Guilty of murder in the first degree and we stress the penalty of death."

A ghastly smile covered Lara's lips.

Judge Wilson rendered the usual speech to the jury and thanked them for their honesty. Lara was again requested to stand.

"We've endeavored, so far as is possible, to give you a fair trial before a jury of your countrymen. The evidence has been such as to satisfy a jury of twelve men, beyond a reasonable doubt, that you've committed the crime of murder, willfully and maliciously. The court has but one course to pursue. . ." the judge announced.

The judge inquired if Lara had anything to say in his own defense.

"I am not guilty," he told listeners in a tone which was nearly inaudible.

"Is there anything more you wish to say?"

"I am not guilty. There is no reason why I should suffer death."

Again he was asked the same question.

"No!"

"The judgment and sentence of the court is that you, Ruperto Lara, on Thursday, the 20th day of April, 1885, be hanged by the neck until your body be dead. And may God have mercy on your soul."

Maximo Apodaca was asked to stand. The charge of murdering the girl was read.

"How do you plead?"

"Guilty!"

"In what degree?"

"In first degree."

Apodaca was asked if he completely understood the weight of his plea. Judge Wilson instructed Col. Fountain to speak privately with Apodaca and tutor him. The two men stepped into a back room.

"It's true," Fountain told the courtroom full of spectators, "he committed the murder, that he did it willfully, that he's told the precise truth and that ever since the perpetration of that deed, his conscience has been a burden to him. He knows that he merits the punishment of death, but that he repents of his crime and wished further time to make his peace with his God.

"His desire," Fountain continued, "is to be allowed to pass the few miserable days or years that God may allow him to live, within the walls of a prison. He asks that the court, it if has the power to influence, to effect this. That such power may be exercised in his behalf."

The court agreed to give consideration to Apodaca's motion. However, the court had no other option but to sentence Apodaca — professed child killer, to be hanged on April 30, 1885.

His sentence was commuted to life in prison by Governor L. A. Sheldon on April 16, 1885.

On April 30, Ruperto Lara, before a crowd of nearly 1200 spectators, heard his last sound on earth. It was the instant his breath was yanked from his lungs as his dangling body hung kicking and gurgling in the mid-afternoon New Mexico sun.

Black Coat

He left behind his own confession as to the murder of the George Nesmith family. It differed somewhat from Apodaca's confession.

Apodaca was sent to the state prison in Santa Fe and became prisoner number 39. He showed signs of mental disturbance right from the start. He was often seen talking to himself and would wake up at night screaming. When asked what was wrong, he would tell his guards that he could "still hear that little girl crying."

On the morning of Nov. 4, 1885, Maximo Apodaca, a butcherer of innocent children, ". . .suddenly leaped from the corridor leading to the fourth tier of cells." Down, down, down his body plunged. His arms flailed outward in search of something to grasp as though he'd changed his mind. But it was too late. When he hit the stone flagging, some 60 feet below the fourth tier, his body bounced and lay still.

He was "fearfully crushed." An inquest was held and his body was buried in a pauper's field near the prison.

The *Rio Grande Republican*, on November 7, 1885, headlined the report of his death "Finis!" The article contained one sentence, "The murder of the Nesmith family is now avenged!"[4]

The Haunting Confession of Ruperto Lara

"When the sun set last Wednesday night," Ruperto Lara knew he'd never live to see another, yet he slept in his cell as usual, indifferent to his fate![1]

April 30, 1885 was the date mass-murderer Ruperto Lara met his fate.

Doña Ana County Sheriff Eugene Van Patten entered the area where the prisoner was held. "Anything special you want for breakfast, Lara?" he asked the prisoner in Spanish.

"Some frijoles con chili is all right." The food was brought and eaten. Lara dressed in a black suit someone had given him. He laid back down on his cot and waited.

Lara was described as "about 30 years old, small in stature, with a scar across his face and projecting teeth which gave him a hardened look. He was a Pueblo Indian" and his manner was said to be "cool and indifferent." He was even called "stoic."

At fifteen minutes after two o'clock p.m., Sheriff Van Patten brought Lara out of his cell and into the vestibule. His arms were bound as he walked beside the sheriff.

"You want a drink of whiskey?"

"I do not need it," Lara replied proudly. "But I will drink it!" He did.

A procession formed with Lara at the head. To his right stood Sheriff Van Patten, and on his left, Deputy Guadalupe Ascarte. Behind them formed a collection of persons from local officials, assistants, press, and an armed militia. The solemn march lasted only two hundred feet before Lara found himself face-to-face with the gallows' jaws of death.

Haunting

Not unlike a conquering hero, Lara stood proudly before the 1,200 spectators and eyed everyone as Sheriff Van Patten read the death warrant.

"Do you have anything to say?"

He did. Daniel Frietze interpreted. Lara re-stated what he'd said earlier in "his full confession."

"Revenge," stated the *Rio Grande Republican*, "seemed uppermost in his mind."

Another delay, due to the non-appearance of the priest who was to officiate the spectacle, came after Lara had finished his confession. Lara's position did not change nor did his face reveal any sign of emotion.

"The prisoner wishes me to tell you people that he does not fear death," Van Patten told the sightseers after Lara had whispered something to him.

About five minutes before Father Monforth arrived, Lara was given another drink of whiskey. Monforth demanded, and was granted, a request that he and Lara be allowed to re-enter the jail. Lara deserved to give his confession in private. Ten minutes later, Monforth and Lara returned to the platform at the hangman's scaffold.

Monforth was requested to ask the prisoner a question.

"Have you ever been asked by any person to make a confession?"

"I've not been advised by anyone to say what I have said," he answered in Spanish.

The priest performed his ceremony. The prisoner watched with interest as the deputies bound his legs and arms more securely. Van Patten placed a black velvet cap over Lara's head and pulled the cap over the Indian's face. Then, the sheriff stepped off the trap door. Lara took a deep breath. Van Patten dropped his handkerchief as a signal.

Lara heard the trap door open its jaws. For one nuclear second, he knew there was nothing to support the weight of sinew and bones. His breath was yanked from the bowels of his dangling body as he now hung – kicking and gurgling in the mid-afternoon New Mexico sun.

His legacy included the murder of George Nesmith, his wife, their 10 year-old daughter, and this "full-confession."

Mr. George Butschofsky, the court interpreter, a representative from the *Rio Grande Republican*, Sheriff Van Patten, and

Col. Albert Fountain of Mesilla, all heard this confession as it was recorded.

"I, Ruperto Lara, am a prisoner in the jail at Las Cruces, under sentence of death for the murder of George Nesmith and his family. My time is very short, and I've not long to live.

"Before I die I want to tell all about the murder of Nesmith and his family and how it was that I was induced to commit that crime. I thought I had some friends who'd help me in this trouble as they promised, but as it appears they have abandoned me to my fate, it is right that I should now speak and tell the truth."

Lara emphasized that his was the whole truth because he was the one about to stand "in the presence of God who will judge [him] for [his] deeds."

He drew attention to the fact that a man named Pat Coghlan lived in Tularosa and that "it is him who got me into this trouble.

"A short time before this thing happened, I was at Coghlan's store in Tularosa. There was present a man whose name I don't know, an American about the size of Mr. Fountain with a reddish or florid complexion and reddish hair and beard or mustache.

"Coghlan and this man talked about two hours while I was there. I bought some provisions and started off. When I was getting on my horse, Coghlan came out of the store and said he wanted to talk to me." Lara then related this story.

"Do you know George Nesmith?" Coghlan inquired.

"No," Lara told him.

"Nesmith lives at Three Rivers on a ranch and has been trying to jump my land at Three Rivers, also. If you'd kill Nesmith for me then I'd pay you for it."

"I can't do it, mister. I've got family living at White Oaks."

"That makes no difference. I'm wanting to find somebody to kill George Nesmith and I'd pay them for it," Coghlan kept stressing.

"I just can't do the job on account of my family."

"Nobody need know anything about it!" Coghlan seemed more than anxious to hire Lara.

"I can't do it! I don't know where Nesmith's ranch is and I don't know him."

Coghlan pulled out a bottle of whiskey from his coat and tossed it to Lara who caught it, took a swallow, and handed it back.

"Keep it. It's for you." The two returned to the store and began to talk seriously about the killing of George Nesmith.

"I'll give you $1,000 to kill Nesmith," Coghlan offered.

Lara then told Fountain and the others that Coghlan had also offered him Nesmith's wagon and horses, which were worth about $300. He stated that he was also given his pick of saddles in Coghlan's store and that he chose "a steel-tree one covered with leather with saddle bags." He gave the saddle away to Mr. Brigido in Barrial, El Paso, Mexico.

Coghlan, Lara confessed, told him to go to the house of a Negro carpenter who lived at Three Rivers. He described the place in detail and said that he was to meet with a man named Pomposo. He would recognize the man in that he had his little finger cut off. Pomposo was supposed to fill Lara in on the rest of the details and point out Nesmith to him.

Afterwards, he was to return to Tularosa. Lara told Coghlan that he'd stay with Henriques Olgin when he returned.

He set out on his journey. While at the carpenter's house, and quite by accident, Nesmith stopped off to speak with Pomposo. Lara just happened to be standing there at the time.

Lara added that it was about this time that he was riding with a partner named Maximo Apodaca. The two of them stopped at the reservation and saw Carlos Martinez. They spent three days with him. When it was time to leave, Lara suggested that Apodaca leave his horse, and he did. This way, he told Apodaca, you'll be afoot when we meet up with Nesmith. From here they traveled back to Tularosa and stayed with Olgin for three more days before word came that it was time to fulfill the contract.

Lara then told the sheriff and Fountain that when word came he was only given $10 in gold and told he'd get the rest when the job was completed. He added that this was the first time he'd told Apodaca they were going to kill Nesmith and his family. He added that he hated to do it because of the little girl.

"That makes no difference," Apodaca told him. "I'll attend to the child myself. The signal should be a shot."

It was settled then. Lara admitted they'd passed only one wagon but said it was "the mail carrier coming from Las Cruces in company with an Indian.

"Every little while," Lara continued, "Maximo would turn around and look back at me as if he were expecting a signal. When I thought we were about half way on the road and it was getting toward sundown, I rode up to the side of the wagon and fired.

"I don't know whether I hit Nesmith or not, but he raised up and halloed. My horse got frightened at the shot and jumped about.

"Maximo got up on the seat, and with his rifle, shot Nesmith in the breast, and he fell. The shots were fired in such quick succession that I couldn't bring my horse up close to the wagon.

"The woman," Lara paused, "crawled under the seat. Maximo placed his rifle under her arm and shot her through. The child was crying. Maximo raised her up and put the rifle at her forehead and shot her."

Lara rode on ahead, he confessed, and Maximo followed in the wagon. They turned off the road and drove until they could not be seen. The spoils were divided and the pair of assassins rode off toward Organ, New Mexico.

After Lara bought some canned meat in Organ, the two rode on toward Santa Barbara and then to El Paso. On their way, Lara said, they passed an ambulance full of soldiers.

"I wanted Maximo to go back with me to Tularosa to get our pay, but he was afraid to go. So I went back by myself. When I got to Tularosa, I went straight to Coghlan's store. Up to that time the killing of Nesmith hadn't been discovered, so far as I know. I told Coghlan that the thing was done just as he wished it.

"He then took me out under a tree, on the corner opposite the store, where we could talk. I told him they were all dead. Then he asked me how the thing had been done. I told him just how it had happened. I told him everything and I said, 'I want you to do what you promised to do.'"

"'I don't know whether this is true!'" Coghlan told Lara. "'How do I know whether they are dead or not?' They may have gone to Franklin. The wife of George Nesmith has relations there."

"Then I told him," Lara confessed, "if he wanted to satisfy himself about it he could go with me and I would show him the place and the bodies."

"'You go and get your partner and bring him back with you. Then I will settle with both of you together'," Coghlan told Lara.

Lara then described the events which took him back to Apodaca. Fountain and Sheriff Van Patten listened with great intent and the reporters took down every word for the record.

Haunting

"What happened when you met up with Apodaca again?" Fountain asked Lara.

"He asked me if I'd got the money from Coghlan. I told him no; that on account of his absence, Coghlan refused to pay it, and I wanted him to go up with me and get our money. But I couldn't induce him to do so.

"From that time afterwards, I never crossed into the United States until Jim Lloyd fooled me into coming over by pretending he wanted me to go into a cattle stealing operation. He put up a job on me and caught me."

Those words ended the "full particulars and his full confession."

If this was the truth, why did Governor L. A. Sheldon sign the papers to reduce Apodaca's sentence to life in prison? Why did he not do the same for Ruperto Lara? Which one of the two told the truth? Which one lied?

Was there a bounty offered for the murder of George Nesmith because of a land squabble? Did Lara actually get paid the money and then try to hold out on Apodaca?

This much we know. Lara was brought out to identify Coghlan from a group of men. He picked H. J. Cuniffe instead. Did Coghlan make some gesture to Lara which caused Lara to fear identifying him? Had someone else posed as Coghlan?

Lara persisted in saying that Coghlan had spoken to him in Spanish every time. It was claimed by others that he knew very little of the language. When asked to pick the "red-faced, florid man," Lara selected Dave Woods, apparently an innocent man in the line-up.

None of the other people implicated by Lara were ever placed on trial. Apodaca wasn't hanged but spent the remainder of his short life in prison. Lara was hanged and left behind his testimony; a testimony filled with just enough detail, just enough theory, and just enough reality that it could be hauntingly true.

Four Sevens and a Sixgun

During 1849, an unknown Mexican discovered a silver lode on the west flank of the Organ Mountains. The location looked down toward Las Cruces. A short time later, Hugh Stephenson, a prospector, became his partner, and a few years later the sole owner. They named their town San Augustine.[1]

Stephenson later sold the mine to Bennett, an officer stationed at Fort Fillmore, for the sum of $12,500.

By 1884 the community boasted the Davis Lesinsky & Co. General Store, a hotel operated by H. M. Foster, a couple of cattle companies, McClary's Saloon, and a population of over one hundred people. Five years later, the Stephenson-Bennett mine, which had produced $1.2 million in silver and lead, played out. The people scattered and San Augustine became one of today's many ghost towns .

But, during the days of the town's glory, it knew its share of "wild west sagas." One such event took place on Wednesday night, December 27, 1882. It happened at the McClary Saloon and had all the earmarks of a real shoot'em up, just like those witnessed on today's silver screen. Even the names of the participants ring true to the old west.[2]

Three cowboys and a Chinaman sat around a poker table on that December night in 1882. The clock on the wall next to the door revealed the hour was about eleven o'clock. Only one man was winning with any regularity and that man was William Burr.

Burr was a buckboard driver during the day and hailed from the nearby town of Tularosa, New Mexico Territory. He regarded himself as an expert poker player and was a frequent winner.

Four Sevens

The Chinaman and another player remain unnamed. The fourth player at the table that particular night was a cowboy whose handle was Santa Cruz Smith. Smith was a local man who worked for Rose and Forster.

Shortly after eleven o'clock that night, Smith and the Chinaman accused Burr of cheating. Burr denied the charge until they discovered two aces hidden inside his coat sleeve.

This broke up the game for the evening. Burr stepped up to the bar and ordered himself a drink. Smith, foaming at the mouth with anger, stormed out of the saloon and went back to his room.

About ten minutes later Smith returned to the saloon, challenged Burr to another hand and the game was soon underway. The chips quickly began to pile up in the middle of the table as each felt he had the winning hand.

Finally, Smith called. Burr spread his cards and revealed he was holding four sevens.

"You're a low-down, dirty, double-dealing cheat." One could almost hear Smith, as he again accused Burr of cheating.

Four Sevens

Burr denied the charge but made no effort to defend his honor with his sixgun.

Smith picked up his money and witnesses heard him exclaim that he'd "see if he did not get that money back." He again left the saloon and returned to his room.

There he packed his belongings and made ready for a quick escape. About an hour or so later, Smith returned to McClary's Saloon.

"Are you going to give me that dollar?" he hollered at Burr after he entered the batwing doors. He pulled his sixgun and pointed it at Burr.

Burr, standing by the end of the bar, was too startled to respond.

"You son-of-a-bitch!" Smith again shouted at Burr."I asked you if you were going to give me back that dollar."

Burr started to turn away from Santa Cruz. Seeing Burr's insolence, Smith squeezed off a shot and the bullet struck Burr in the chest. He staggered backwards and began to fall. Smith fired a second shot. Burr's head exploded as the bullet pierced his brain. He was dead.

Smith fired a third shot which missed Burr and entered the saloon wall. Then, still holding his sixgun with his right hand, Smith ran out the batwing doors and headed for the corral. Two men stood near the corral and helped Smith load his belongings upon his horse and watched him ride away.

As news spread throughout the mining town about the shooting, several miners learned about the two men who'd assisted Smith in his flight. The miners demanded that the two men be expelled from the town − by force if necessary. This feeling soon passed and the men's mood softened.

The local stage coach driver, referred to only as Charley, was called upon to follow Santa Cruz Smith and arrest him. After all, the townspeople insisted, Charley had been a deputy sheriff up until his recent resignation. Charley refused.

One miner suggested they contact Mr. B. E. Davies, also a former deputy sheriff. They tried. The man who answered the knock at Mr. Davies' door felt it useless to try and follow Smith's trail at that hour of night. Therefore, he did not disturb Mr. Davies and the latter was unaware of the murder until the following morning.

What were the miners going to do?

Four Sevens

Mr. Hamilton, the newly elected constable, was in Las Cruces. Even the Justice of the Peace, Mr. Forster, refused to do anything.

And what about the county sheriff?

"Sheriff Bull has not moved in the matter!" the reporter was quick to add.

They buried nineteen year-old William Burr the following Friday. Nearly every miner in the camp attended the funeral — every miner except Santa Cruz Smith.

As for Smith, he faded into the lost annals of the history of the old west.

The newspaper called for the miners of the town to elect "some good man as Marshal to enforce order in the camp. We know a man now in camp who will just suit them. A man who brought order out of anarchy in Lake Valley in its early days. A man who has received many encomiums, as well as scars, with the lightness and ease with which he handles his six-shooter. We need hardly say that his name is Mr. McDougall.

"Now, what are we going to do?" the editor concluded.

Shootout in Cotton's Saloon

George W. Lufkin, a cowboy, first discovered silver ore in 1878. The location of his find became the town of Lake Valley, New Mexico Territory. When his rock ore was evaluated, it assayed high in content; yet, Lufkin received a mere $10.50 from the sale of the property.

According to James E. Sherman, in his book, *Ghost Towns and Mining Camps of New Mexico*,[1] Lufkin's discovery was "very near to where the celebrated Bridal Chamber" was located. The Bridal Chamber, yielded over three million dollars in silver.

In the early 1880s, two miners struck an ore vein which they sold for $100,000. Again, according to Sherman, "two days after the sale, it was discovered that the ore vein ran into a subterranean room." That room was named the Bridal Chamber. The sad part of the tale is that on the same day of this discovery in 1881, George Daly, the mine owner, was massacred by Apache Indians.

The town officially started in September of 1882. It was named after a small lake in the immediate area which later went dry. Before long, it boasted stamp mills, three churches, smelting works, two weekly newspapers, a school, shops, stores, hotels, and a thousand people – most of whom found themselves in the numerous saloons whenever possible.

It was in one of these, Cotton's Saloon, on December 30, 1883 that this story took place.

Cowboy Dan McCabe was getting an early start on the New Year celebration. He'd already consumed a considerable amount of whiskey and was feeling like God had created the earth just for him to roam. He'd been told several times to cease his "boisterous and unseemly language," but refused.

The bartender, realizing there was nothing else to do but send for the sheriff, finally withdrew and did so. He went to the E. Ford home, "who was acting as deputy marshal in place of

Roberts, who was sick." Ford grabbed his sixgun and the leather crackled as he strapped it about his waist. Both men headed for Cotton's Saloon.

Ford paused just outside the batwing saloon doors and looked in to see what was going on. Then he entered. He walked up to McCabe, who was standing at the bar, and ordered him to stop his disruptive actions immediately. The drunken cowboy demanded to know just who it was that was going to make him.

Silence, the thickness of a New Mexico sandstorm, blew into the saloon. Spectators could hear the wall clock ticking. Behind the saloon a dog yelped. Ford stared at McCabe and neither man spoke.

Then, with his left hand, Ford reached out to take McCabe's sixgun from his holster. McCabe knocked it away and stepped back, all in the same move. Ford's right shoulder flinched as his hand went down for the Colt revolver that hugged his hip. McCabe drew.

A bursting flash of light extended from the barrel tip of McCabe's sixgun. The bullet went wild. He fired a second time.

Ford felt the bite of the bullet as it ripped away at his left hand. His gun was out, too.

Several shots were fired.

Then, as quickly as it had started, it was over. Ford stood leaning against the bar, his left hand a bloody mess, and McCabe sprawled upon the sawdust floor. The front of his shirt was soaked with his own blood. His Colt revolver, was still clutched in his right hand as a trickle of gun smoke slithered skyward from the barrel. He was dead.

The reporter wasn't bashful about telling his readers that as the bartender cleaned up, "several ears, noses and fingers not identified, though some of them may have been relics of former fights" were found upon the floor of the saloon.

The following day a jury trial was held before Justice Russell. The jury returned a verdict of justifiable homicide.

Shootouts, such as this one in Cotton's Saloon, must have been rather common-place. The reporter noted the jury was then "discharged for a few hours to wait for the next shooting scrape."[2]

Sin, Sex, and a Shooting

It's an old saying that if there were no money and no women in the world, we could do away with all our judges, juries, lawyers and courts of justice. It is certain that nine tenths of the crimes committed by humanity have their inspiration from one or the other source."[1]

This was the opening paragraph for a lustful, Old West murder newspaper story titled SHOOTING AT ORGAN! The location was the mining camp of Organ, New Mexico, located in the Organ Mountains east of Las Cruces.

Several social and moral issues arose as a result of this incident. "Just how far a man shall approach a woman, and still keep within the bounds of the law and exactly what constitutes a deadly insult to a woman, justifying the husband or nearest relative taking the law into his own hands, and slaying the offender either at the instant or when he next meets him, is a question which this trial will go far to decide – at least in this Territory."

Everything came to a head on May 2, 1883. Van Elliott and his brother Robert worked a mine at Quartzite Mountain. It was a five-mile ride by horseback to their home in Organ where Mrs. Van Elliott was doing her chores.

As usual, Sam Hester spent the morning delivering water in his wagon. He made his living by driving to the spring, located three miles from Organ, and taking water back to the mining camp in the mystical Organ Mountains.

On this particular Wednesday morning, Hester took extra-special notice of Mrs. Elliott; in particular, the way in which her clothes seemed to lend themselves to her youthful figure –

embracing her. 'If she were to release her hair in the breeze, she'd be more beautiful,' he no doubt fantasized.

But he said nothing. Instead, he suppressed his desires into the half-hearted task of peddling water. He climbed back aboard his wagon and rode away.

As he continued his rounds, he could feel the fire burning up within him to make love with Mrs. Elliott. He rationalized his actions as he spoke out loud to himself.

"Shortly after," the newspaper recorded, "he returned to Mrs. Elliott's house. . . ."

He entered through the back door and stepped lightly to where Mrs. Elliott sat. She, no doubt, inquired as to the reason for his return. The sullen Hester determined he was going to have Mrs. Elliott − one way or another!

This man, who'd been without a woman for a long time, made his move. Not to what degree he advanced, but merely that he moved, is all we're told.

The sound of Mrs. Elliott's hand when it connected with his face there in the tiny house must have bitterly shattered his ego. He stopped!

She glared!

"Don't tell anyone!" he warned her. He nodded and walked back out the door.

Mrs. Elliott ran out the front door. He heard the slam even from behind the house as she headed across the road. She went toward Mr. Kennedy's restaurant. The molester drew his sixgun and fired. Mrs. Elliott heard him shout some obscenity at her as the bullet missed. She later claimed it "intimidated her."

Once inside, she related all the particulars as to what and how it had happened. Mr. Kennedy listened intently.

The next morning, and why they waited that long is uncertain, they sent word to her husband at the mine. He and his brother wasted no time in traveling the five miles to their home.

Van tried to comfort his wife. As the evening wore on, the two Elliotts plotted their attack. They would wait until morning, and then −.

The following morning, Friday, May 4th, Hester again made his water run. With him sat George Haney. Both sat erect as the wagon pulled up in front of Kennedy's. Each carried a pistol and a Winchester rifle.

Across the road, also armed, Van and Robert watched from inside their cabin. Van held onto his favorite shotgun and Robert carried a new revolver he'd only shot five times since he bought it.

Hester stepped down from the wagon and began unloading Kennedy's water. Robert came out of the cabin. Van followed.

"I want you to go. . ." Robert hollered.

Like the tail of a dust-devil, Hester's hand went down; and, with tornado-like force, his sixgun whipped upwards into his palm. He pointed it at Robert's chest. It was fully cocked.

Robert leaped backwards. Concerned about the safety of his brother, Van, who'd been viewing it all, brought his shotgun up on Hester. He'd rehearsed the move a dozen times while fighting Indians or hunting wild turkey. The big gun kicked when he pulled the trigger.

Robert and Hester also fired during this time.

Hester was first to feel the lightning heat of a bullet pass through him as he caught one in the side. He fell sideways but continued to fire his weapon.

Haney, who was still in the wagon, now stood and fired. Suddenly, a bullet caught him in his right wrist. His gun went hurtling away.

Van Elliott, who's shot had not hit Hester because he was too far away, had his coat sleeve vented by a .44 that passed through on its way to a nearby wooden post. He fired again.

Hester went down. There was a crimson hole in his back.

It didn't take the spring winds long to clear away the gun smoke. Spectators started to gather. Several men picked up Hester and carried him into Shryock's Saloon.

Dr. Bogart checked Hester and then attended to Haney's wounds. Hester, he'd concluded, would have to wait on Dr. Burt's more capable hands. Dr. Burt had further to travel to reach the shootout site.

Hester hovered between life and death until around 4 a.m. Sunday morning. His life's blood flowed off the table and dropped onto the sawdust floor. He died lying on a saloon table.

Meanwhile, following the shooting, Robert and Van turned themselves over to Mr. Joblin — the local lawman. They told him they had shot Haney and Hester. He listened and then told them to go home. But, he reminded them, they were to consider themselves under arrest.

They did.

Judge Valdez called the hearing to order on Monday, May 7, 1883. It concluded on the 9th. Col. William L. Rynerson and his assistant, Mr. Wade, defended the Elliott brothers. Judge Simon B. Newcomb handled the prosecution.

Newcomb tried to substantiate the fact that Hester had been shot in the back. He was convinced, he told the jury, that the brothers entered the restaurant and killed Hester while he was carrying a bucket of water in his right hand. "He had no chance whatever to defend himself," Newcomb told the court.

Additional testimony presented evidence that Hester "was somewhat of a boisterous character, fond of firing his pistol and halloing in the streets, though there's nothing very bad on record against him."

The Elliotts, on the other hand, were portrayed as two young men who went to work, paid their bills, and lived a quiet and peaceful life. They rarely "carried weapons and still more rarely indulged in quarreling of any kind.

"Though it was colored somewhat by their individual feelings," continued the reporter, "the witnesses gave their testimony clearly and with the evident intention of telling the truth."

Despite the eloquent speeches, the witness accounts which supported the Elliotts, and some other extremely important facts, Van and Robert were held over for District Court and a $4,000 bond placed on each of the brothers.

Time, being a cruel master and combined with human abuse, has caused the loss of the records. What happened next? Everything points to the fact that Van and Robert were released. Even the El Paso, Texas paper picked up on the story and called for the brothers' release.

"The question before the camp [is] whether or not it is safe for a lady to remain there under the shadow of her own home," concluded the editor of the *Rio Grande Republican*. "Or whether she is to be exposed to insult from any one who chooses to enter her doors by the back way.

"Should the result of the trial be in anywise doubtful on this point, the result will be that every honest female will immediately disappear from among them, and the effect will be disastrous to the infant city. Is this what the people of Organ desire?"

How would you have voted if you'd been on the jury? Remember, your vote could make a difference whether the women stayed or left!

Col. Fountain and the Ghost of Ruidoso

One of the most eerie ghost tales, especially for persons familiar with southern New Mexico history, is the one involving Col. Albert J. Fountain of La Mesilla, and the Ghost of Ruidoso.

The story began in the 1870s "when John Chisum of the Jingle Bob Ranch, South Spring, New Mexico, made decoys out of several oversized bull mavericks, branded with the rail brand."[1]

A short time later, Bob Ollinger found one of these bulls roaming the New Mexico Territory, roped him, and rebranded him with "the skull and bones brand, named him Ruidoso and put a curse on him."

There followed a string of tragedies which were always accompanied by the presence of the bull. One of these was the Lincoln County War, "in which Ollinger himself was killed by Billy the Kid during the latter's escape from the Lincoln County jail."

Clay Allison's death was also attributed to Ruidoso when the bull appeared and spooked Allison's team into a stampede.

In 1888, the eleven year-old bull became public property and was condemned to be auctioned. At that time, Col. Jack Potter met the bull.

"After finding out that I was the only trail boss that would volunteer to take old Ruidoso to the shipping point," he wrote in his story, "I went over to the herd and contacted [Ruidoso]."

Potter related how he talked to the bull, calling him "an old outlaw devil," and telling the bull he'd not come to cuss him but

Col. Albert Jennings Fountain

to lecture him. He related Ruidoso's story to the bull and challenged the bull to "behave yourself and not start anything."

The trail drive began and no incident occurred. The herd arrived in Amarillo, Texas, "a new town built down in a lake bed," and Ruidoso was placed aboard a train headed for the L. A. Allen Livestock Commission Company in Kansas City." Ten hours out of Amarillo, the train wrecked and Ruidoso escaped.

"This was a curse on Amarillo and the next year its location was moved to the present site," Potter said. People all over the territory began to believe that Ruidoso "was connected with the devil."

No one knows for sure when Ruidoso died, however, his ghost began to make public appearances all over the New Mexico Territory. He was seen and heard to bellow "from Monnihan Wells on the Staked Plains to Anton Chico on the Pecos."

"The climax of this ghost steer's career came one night in the neighborhood of Blazer's Mills," according to James Monaghan in *The Book of the American West.*

At this point, Col. A. J. Fountain entered the ghost story. With the aid of his chief investigator, Ben Williams, Col. Fountain accumulated enough evidence to prosecute Doña Ana County cattle rustlers Oliver Lee, Jim Gilliland, Billy McNew and Joe Morgan.[2] He left his home in Mesilla, accompanied by his youngest child, in January, 1896 for a trial in Lincoln, New Mexico.[3]

He finished his business on Thursday, January 30th. He loaded the buckboard, added his young son, Henry, said good-bye to a few friends in Lincoln and began the long journey to Mesilla and home.

They arrived in Mescalero, eighteen miles from Lincoln, and decided to spend the night. The following morning, Fountain and his son hitched up the team and headed out on the Tularosa road for Las Cruces.

"He met a number of vehicles and horsemen," A. M. Gibson says in his biography of Fountain. "Several of the travelers he knew and he pulled up a number of times for a chat."

That night, the Col. and young Henry slept in La Luz, New Mexico. Like all children, young Henry had a sweet tooth so his father gave him a quarter to spend at Myers' store.

Ghost of Ruidoso

The following morning, Fountain and young Henry once more headed down the road toward home. By noon they arrived at the eastern edge of the eerie and mysterious White Sands. There they rested the team and ate dinner. By three o'clock, they were nearing a place on the east side of the Organ Mountains called Chalk Hill.

"An old Mescalero buck stopped them and told them he had heard the Ghost Steer bellow for three nights over toward Blazer's Mill and the burial ground.[4] And just the previous night a light flashed over the reservation to the west and in that flash could be seen the images of the ghost [of Ruidoso], Bob Ollinger, and Buckshot Roberts." Roberts also died in the Lincoln County War.

The Mescalero warned Col. Fountain not to continue his journey as the "Indians in that vicinity were highly superstitious."

"The Colonel laughed at the Indian's warning and went on his way."

No one can say for sure if the ghostly warnings had anything to do with what happened next. But one thing is historically true, "That was the last time Col. Fountain and his son were seen alive. The tragedy of their disappearance is still unsolved!"

The Ghost of Billy's Killer

"Pat's [Garrett] death was one of the unsolved mysteries of the southwest," a reporter, believed to be Allen Papen, told author Margaret P. Hood. "Some old-timers still think Brazel didn't kill him, that Pat was the victim of a closely worked out plot."[1]

If what Papen told Ms. Hood was fact, then who really killed Pat Garrett? If there was a plot, and such is very possible, then who was behind the conspiracy? And, what was the reason for killing the man who'd become famous for shooting down one of the West's most popular criminals – Billy the Kid?

Further, why is so very little attention given to the fact that Pat Garrett's ghost made an appearance on the day of his death! Why indeed?

Let's take a close look at the facts!

History records that Garrett shot Billy the Kid in July of 1881. From that instant, Pat Garrett was a nationally-known figure.

On Thursday, January 30, 1896, Col. Albert J. Fountain stopped at the home of Dr. J. H. Blazer, as the former headed back home from the Lincoln County court. While visiting with the doctor, Fountain told "how he'd secured indictments against a gang of cattle rustlers and said he had enough evidence to convict the whole gang if they didn't make away with him or the witnesses."[2] One gang member was the infamous Oliver Lee. Fountain and his son never made it home, but were presumably murdered on the trail.

Later that same year Garrett ran for Sheriff of Doña Ana County. He based his campaign on the promise that he would

79

Billy's Killer

Sheriff Patrick Floyd Garrett

get Col. Fountain's killers and bring them to justice. He won the election.

"Col. Fountain's friends pushed Garrett to act, for, as they pointed out, every day, week, year of delay was an advantage to the side of the Colonel's killers."

Two years later, Garrett brought the suspected murderers to trial. Oliver Lee, Jim Gilliland and Billy McNew stood trial before Judge Frank W. Parker and were acquitted. Garrett was furious and swore he'd not give up.

He'd failed to keep his campaign promise. Yet, he had "the reputation of never letting up on a trail once he got the whiff of a wrong-doer." Therefore, it was almost certain that he never ceased to gather evidence, perhaps in secret, to convict Oliver Lee and his notorious gang.

In 1901, President Theodore Roosevelt appointed Garrett Collector of Customs at El Paso, Texas.[4] Some time later, Pat and Tom Powers, owner of the Coney Island Saloon in El Paso, attended a Rough Riders convention in San Antonio. Garrett convinced Roosevelt that Powers was the "biggest cattleman in West Texas." Because of this flim-flam, the President allowed Powers to pose with him for a picture. Shortly thereafter Roosevelt learned Garrett had lied to him.

"When Roosevelt learned that he had his picture taken with a saloonkeeper, and that Pat was responsible for the *lese majeste*, he was through with Garrett." Garrett served four years in his post but President Roosevelt refused to reappoint him.

It was about this time that Garrett mortgaged two of his ranches to Martin Lohman for $3,567.50, but failed to repay the note when due. On April 13, 1905, Lohman sold the note to William W. Cox — Garrett's neighbor and secret enemy. What followed became known as 'Garrett's most deadly feud.' Cox confiscated several head of Pat's cattle and refused to return them until Pat repaid the note.[5]

Cox was no longer a secret enemy, but instead, publicly denounced Garrett on several occasions. All of Doña Ana County knew about the feud between the two ranchers.[6]

It wasn't long before word went around about a "secret meeting" at the St. Regis Hotel in El Paso. Those in attendance were Oliver Lee, Billy McNew, a Texas gunman, Jim Miller, Carl Adamson, Wayne Brazel and W. W. Cox. "Cox supposedly called this group together because he feared that Garrett was getting too close to solving the Fountain mystery.

William Webb Cox

Cox agreed to pay for the shooting but insisted that the murder had to appear as self-defense. Lee finally came up with the most acceptable solution. He suggested that Wayne Brazel lease the unused Bear Canyon Ranch [owned by Garrett] and put goats on it. When Garrett complained, the ensuing dispute would provide an excuse to kill him.

Most people could be counted on to be sympathetic to Brazel, and if he took the blame for the killing, a jury would certainly free him. Since Brazel wasn't a professional gunman and might himself be killed if he tried to shoot Garrett, someone else would have to do the job and guarantee its effectiveness."[7]

On March 11, 1907, Jesse Wayne Brazel leased the land from the Pat Garrett family. The lease was for five years. Nothing was said about turning loose a herd of goats on the range.

Wayne, the son of Jesse M. Brazel, was born in 1876 at Greenwood City, Kansas.[8] Although the family lived in Eagle Creek, New Mexico Territory sometime later, there is no evidence showing they were the same Brazel's involved in the Lincoln County War. Later, the Brazel family moved to Cold Camp which bordered the San Augustine Ranch owned by W. W. Cox. Cox took an instant liking to the blue-eyed, good-natured boy "who wore his wide-brimmed sombrero pulled tightly down across his ears."

Dependability and loyalty were inbred in young Wayne. Most sources agreed that the youth worshiped Cox. He would have died for him, and, if necessary, would have killed for him.

His likability was such that he was never without work. He didn't drink and was known for his honesty. He handled the toughest jobs and never complained. Cox often used the lad to break wild horses out at his ranch.

Within a week of leasing the Garrett ranch, young Brazel herded 1,800 goats onto the range land. The stage was now set. It was now Pat's move.

It was nearly nine months before Pat took legal action against Wayne. In January, 1908, he went to Las Cruces and obtained a warrant for Brazel's arrest. He charged the youth with a violation of an old statute which forbade keeping livestock within a mile and a half of a ranch house or settlement.

Jesse Wayne Brazel

Billy's Killer

The case went to trial. Garrett failed to obtain a conviction. His temper got the better of him and he was now desperate. Wayne Brazel and his goats had to go before they ruined his range land!

Other things occupied Pat's mind that January. He was an ambitious man and strongly missed the limelight of public office. The need to be in a position of power was like a strong drug within his veins, and he was determined to satisfy his craving no matter what it cost.

Shortly before the end of February, 1908, Pat visited Allen Papen's office to discuss his ambition. He told the editor how he wanted to be sheriff once more and inquired as to what Papen thought of his chances to win. He even mentioned that he felt his luck was beginning to change.[9]

A couple of cowboys, he told Papen, had recently come to him. Carl Adamson and some Texan named Jim Miller wanted to lease his ranch for the purpose of grazing a thousand head of cattle. Miller, it seems, had bought them in Mexico and wanted to graze them for a while in New Mexico before sending them on up the trail to his ranch in Oklahoma.

Miller, Pat told Papen, had even offered to pay Garrett the sum of three thousand dollars for the use of his range land and an additional one dollar per head if Garrett would drive the cattle up from Mexico for him. It was just the kind of luck the hard-drinking, short-tempered Garrett needed at this time.

There was one hitch, however, he told Papen. Pat still had to get rid of Cox's boy, Wayne Brazel. That wasn't going to be easy with Cox being one of the richest cattlemen in southern New Mexico.

Cox's spread, the San Augustine Ranch, was one of the most outstanding cattle ranches in New Mexico. William Webb Cox, sole owner of the 105,000 acres, hailed from DeWitt County, Texas.[10] He was born November 12, 1854. As a young boy, he'd grown up with the fighting and feuding common to Texas in those days. He was just 19 years old when his father, James Webb Cox, was gunned down in an old-west style shootout. He arrived on the scene to find his father riddled with fifty-eight bullets. In the true spirit of the family feud, young William vowed revenge for his father's death.

Young William blamed the gunfighter John Wesley Hardin for his father's death, and for years thereafter, the two were prepared to shoot each other on sight. Twenty-two years later, on August 19, 1895, the infamous John W. Hardin was shot in the back at the Coney Island Saloon in El Paso. The feud was ended.[11]

As a young man, Cox married Margaret Zerilda Rhodes. Her sister, Winnie P. Rhodes, married none other than the outlaw Oliver Lee — the man Garrett had been trying to hang for nearly a decade, and family ties were very close.

It was now Friday, February 28, 1908. Spring was coming to the Mesilla Valley and the whole desert valley was alive with life. The sun was shining brightly that day when Carl Adamson appeared in Las Cruces to rent a buggy for the long, four-hour drive out to the Garrett ranch, where he intended to spend the night.

He arrived that afternoon and was greeted by Pat, his wife, three of their children and cowboys Frank Adams, Tom Emory, and an unidentified Mexican. Pat showed Adamson about the ranch. Besides his boasting, which Garrett was known to do with a flair, he mentioned a disturbance of prowlers from the night before. Adams, the ranch hand, had even found tracks of two riders in an arroyo near the house. Neither man made any reference as to who or what could have caused such a disturbance.

Adamson was a short, stout man with a boyish, intelligent face. His very presence disturbed Mrs. Garrett and later that night, when she was alone with her husband, she mentioned her fears to him. Pat simply laughed and reminded her that their financial worries were soon going to be over.

The next day was leap year day, February 29th. Pat awoke in exceptionally high spirits. The 6'5" Garrett, whose hair was now beginning to whiten about the temples, dressed in his best suit. He chatted happily with his wife and children that morning. Nothing seemed to bother him. It was going to be a beautiful day, he told all.

After breakfast, he and Adamson climbed into the two-horse buggy. He bid his family goodbye and pointed the horses down the lane in the direction of the Organ Mountains and Las Cruces.

"Pauline!" shouted Mrs. Garrett. "Quick, get your horse! Your father has forgotten his topcoat."

The slender, youthful Garrett daughter scrambled aboard the nearby mare and raced out after her father. Pat could hear the galloping of the horse as she neared the buggy. He told

Adamson to hold up a bit so he could see what his daughter wanted.

Carl reined the two horses to a stop and Garrett climbed out of the buggy. Dust drifted upwards from the hoofs of the mare as the young girl brought it to a stop beside the buggy. Pat reached up and pulled his daughter from the back of the mare. He gave her a big hug before lowering her to the ground. She handed him the topcoat and he kissed her on the cheek.

"Take good care of mommy and I will bring you a pretty," he told her as he placed her back on the mare. She promised she would, waved goodbye, and rode back to the house. She was never to feel his touch, never to hear his fatherly voice, never to gaze into his loving eyes again. The man who'd rocked her so many times on his knee would rock her never again. She would never get the "pretty" he promised.

The long, twisting road wound past Gold Camp, through the San Augustine Pass of the Organ Mountains, and into the mining camp of Organ before moving down the valley and into Las Cruces.

Willis Walter, son of Russel Walter who owned the livery stable in Organ, was busy unloading alfalfa when Carl Adamson and Pat Garrett pulled up and stopped. They allowed the horses to drink while they talked among themselves.

"Have you seen Brazel?" Garrett asked Willis, as if he'd been expecting to see him along the road or meet up with him somewhere.

"Yes, he just left," Willis told the two men. He pointed down the road where the dust was being kicked up behind a galloping horse.

The two men chatted a while longer with Willis and then Carl headed the horses down the lane "at a brisk trot."

Below Organ the road forked and became two until the traveler was nearly to Las Cruces. When Garrett and Adamson reached the junction "they saw Brazel a short distance down the Mail-Scott road talking to a stranger. The lone rider split and vanished before" they could reach them.

At last they overtook Brazel. Garrett gave a curt nod as a greeting and the three of them continued on toward Las Cruces.

As the three approached Alameda Arroyo, Brazel shouted at Garrett. It was as though he wanted to signal someone, his voice was so loud.

"If I don't sell the whole bunch, I won't sell none," he screamed in reference to selling his goats.

Adamson halted the team. He climbed from the buggy and walked around in front of the two horses. He maneuvered himself into a position where he might urinate. Pat apparently felt it was as good a time as any to do the same. He climbed from the buggy, stepped to the rear, turned his back on Brazel, removed his left glove and unbuttoned his trousers.

He did not hear the explosion. Instead, he felt the searing penetration of the projectile as it hit him in the back of the head with the force of a mule's kick. The bullet gathered long strands of Pat's graying hair and carried them forward through his brain and out the front of his face near his right eye. His body whirled and his knees sagged under him. He could feel death's hot breath screaming in his ear but no sound came from his lips.

Billy's Killer

The man who'd murdered Billy the Kid in the dark was now lying in the dirt – dead!

It was nearly noon.

Meanwhile, back at the Garrett ranch house, Apolinaria Garrett, Pat's wife, picked up a long, solid-oak board to prop against the door. She prayed for a spring breeze to cool out the hot house.

"We will have a good life when all this is settled," she related to young Pauline.

No dust-devils were blowing, no sand was carried along in a New Mexico dust storm, nothing was stirring. Then, for no apparent reason, the long, solid-oak board "tipped up and over, slamming onto the floor with an ear-shattering noise."

"Something has happened!" Mrs. Garrett began to scream. "I don't know what it is, but something has happened!"

Outside the house the dogs began to howl. Pauline tried to console her mother by assuring her "everything will be all right."

Was Pat's ghost trying to contact them? It was almost noon![12]

Back at the murder scene, Adamson climbed back into the buggy and the two men rode on to town. A few minutes later, with his sixgun in his right hand, Wayne Brazel walked into Sheriff Felipe Lucero's office. He laid the .45 on the desk.

"Lock me up," he said. "I've just killed Pat Garrett!"

Lucero laughed. "What are you trying to do, Wayne, josh me?" he asked.

Brazel persisted.

"The man who was with Pat when I killed him is outside the jail. He's a man named Adamson and he saw the whole thing and knows I shot in self-defense."

The Sheriff picked up the gun and locked it in the safe. Wayne was locked in a cell. Lucero went outside and found Carl Adamson sitting in the buggy. He climbed aboard and they headed east.

Allen Papen, the editor Garrett had talked to a few days earlier, was sitting at his desk. He looked up and saw men running down the street. What he saw had all the earmarks of a good news story. He jumped up and ran to the front door, opened it, and saw Lucero driving hell-bent down Main Street.

"What's up, Felipe?" he shouted.

"Pat Garrett has been killed out on the Organ Road," Lucero shouted back. He slowed the buggy and Papen climbed aboard. This was going to sell newspapers as far away as Chicago and New York. There was no way he was going to miss this chance!

"All I know is that a few minutes ago Wayne Brazel came walking into my office, cool as a cucumber, with a .45 in his hand and told me he'd shot Pat Garrett in self-defense." Lucero continued talking when Papen had seated himself in the buggy alongside Dr. Field.

"I can tell you how it happened," Carl Adamson said, looking back over his shoulder toward Papen. "My partner Miller and I have been dickering with Garrett to run a bunch of cattle on his land. This man Brazel was trying to hold us up to pay a fancy price for a few scrubby goats he's been grazing on this land which he said Garrett had leased to him."[13]

The editor silently recalled his earlier talk with Pat and the names being mentioned were now all too familiar.

"I spent last night at Garrett's ranch," Adamson continued his narrative. "This morning we were driving into town to meet Brazel and try to talk some sense into him. We'd gone a few miles along the road when we heard a horseman coming up behind. It was Brazel."

Carl continued with his long story. He finally concluded. "I turned around in time to see Pat reach into the back of the buggy for his shotgun. At that same time, Wayne pulled his .45 from his waistband of his pants and shot twice."

"Did Pat shoot?" Lucero interrupted Adamson.

"Never had a chance."

"So Brazel shot twice? Where did he hit Pat?" Lucero again interrupted.

"I don't know. I didn't look at the body."

"Weren't much interested, were you?" Lucero grunted, his voice carrying every bit of sarcasm he could muster.

Adamson just stared at him.

A short time later, the men arrived on the scene. They found Pat lying on his back, his eyes open, dead in a six-inch sand dune. His shotgun lay about four feet from his body. Dr. Field, who'd been listening to Adamson's detailed narrative, climbed out of the buggy, walked over to the body and began to examine it.

He found Garrett had been shot twice. One bullet had entered the back of Pat's head and torn itself away at the right eyebrow. The second bullet had penetrated the body from the upper part of the stomach to the upper part of the shoulders. It had remained in the body.

Meanwhile, Sheriff Lucero conducted his own investigation of the event. Lucero traced the buggy's tracks backwards for about two miles and found where a rider had joined the buggy near the old Chalk Hill.

"You, Adamson, you say you got out of the buggy?" Lucero asked, looking at the young man, his black eyes sharp for every detail.

The cowboy nodded.

"From the footprints, I'd say two men got out."

"That's right," Adamson began to stutter. "Garrett got out too."

"So was he on the ground when he was shot?"

"On the ground and reaching into the back of his buggy for his shotgun," Adamson responded.

The men loaded Pat's body into the buggy and headed back to town. At the jail, Carl Adamson repeated his story word for word — as though he'd memorized it.

The next day was Sunday, March 1st. Mrs. Garrett was notified of her husband's death about midnight. Later that morning, she drove the long winding road to town where she viewed her husband's corpse.

Two days later, on Tuesday, Manuel Lopez, Justice of the Peace, called his court of inquiry to order. Wayne Brazel was asked to stand and answer to the charge of murdering Pat Garrett. There was a blank look on his face as the charge was read. He stared for several seconds at nothing in particular before he responded.[14]

"What's that?" he asked.

The charge was repeated.

"Not guilty," he answered. He resumed his seat and the queer look remained on his face.

Mark Thompson conducted the prosecution despite the fact that he was a close friend of Albert B. Fall. Thompson was assisted by New Mexico Attorney General James M. Hervey. Among the lawyers for the defense sat Albert B. Fall. Fall's influence was stronger these days since the strange disappearance of Col. Fountain. Garrett had suspected Fall of being indirectly involved with the Fountains' disappearance.

"Now tell to your best recollection what happened?" Hervey asked Adamson as the latter took the witness stand.

"I stopped the buggy and as I got out Mr. Garrett reached over and took the reins. And while I was standing there I heard Mr. Garrett say, 'Well, damn you. If I don't get you off one way, I will another,' or something like that," Adamson smirked.

"Where were these people in relation to you?" was Adamson's next question.

"Mr. Garrett was in the buggy and Brazel was on his horse. They were at my back."

"So you didn't see Garrett standing upright at all?"

"I think when I seen Garrett the first shot had been fired and he was staggering."

"Did he fall to the side, to the front, or the rear of the buggy?"

"About two feet from the side," came the answer.

"Where was the defendant at this time?"

"He was on horseback, about even with the buggy. He had a sixshooter in his hand."

"Who fired the second shot?"

At this point, Adamson began to avoid answering the questions put to him. Hervey made no effort to get Adamson to answer the questions.

"One of my horses started to run," Carl began to answer. "I grabbed the lines and wrapped them as quickly as I could around the hub of the wheel. I went back to where Mr. Garrett lay."

Such an answer to a simple question would not have made the grade in a court which was honestly searching for the truth to the murder of a man. But in this court, at this time, evasive answers were accepted to important questions.

"Did Garrett speak?" Hervey continued to question Carl Adamson.

"No, when I got to him he was just stretching out. He did groan a little."

Dr. Field was next to testify. He stated his views about the autopsy he'd performed and that, in his opinion, it was "unmistakable evidence that Garrett had been shot from behind." He also "declared unequivocally at the inquest over the body that in

Las Cruces N.M.
Feby 29 1908

We the undersigned Justice of the Peace
and Coroners Jury have attended the
investigation of the body of Pat Garrett
who was reported dead within the
limits of Precinct No 30 county of
Dona Ana & Territory of New Mexico
or about five miles north east of the
town of Las Cruces and find that
the deceased came to his death by
gun shot wounds inflicted by
one Wayne Brazel.

Manuel Lopez
Justice of the Peace Precinct No 2
D. J. Baker Foreman Jury

Hugh Clary.
W B May.
C. S. Pearson
J. F. Faithly
Hay Perry

**Copy of the Autopsy Report on Pat Garrett
Certified by Doña Ana County Clerk's Office**

his opinion the shooting of Pat Garrett was murder in cold blood, murder in the first degree."

On April 13, 1908, the Grand Jury indicted Wayne Brazel for the murder of Pat Garrett. His bond was set at $10,000. Within a matter of minutes, the man who'd sat next to Wayne Brazel throughout the inquest, Mr. W. W. Cox, had posted the bond with the aid of six other men.

Wayne Brazel walked the streets of Las Cruces as a free man for the next year and six days. Finally, after all that time, and all the public demands for a trial, he was brought before Judge Frank W. Parker on April 19, 1909.

Prosecutor Thompson's attitude was one which loudly proclaimed, 'let's hurry and get the damn thing over with.' He subpoenaed telegrams from Western Union which linked Wayne Brazel, Carl Adamson, Jim Miller, W. W. Cox, and A. P. Rhodes in a possible conspiracy; yet, when it came to the trial, he never presented them as evidence.[15] All his efforts were half-hearted at the very best. He made no attempt to dwell on the fact that Pat had been shot in the back of the head. Nor did he undertake to explain why a man would declare "self-defense" for shooting another man while the latter was in the process of urinating. It just didn't seem to make sense. Likewise, no effort was put forth to discuss why Garrett still had his glove on his right hand. After all, if he were fearing an attack, he would have removed the glove so he might fire his own weapon.

Thompson also bungled other strong points throughout the trial. He failed to explain why Pat's shotgun was only loaded with birdshot and not loaded for a possible gunfight with a man. Also regarding the shotgun, he failed to explain the position of the shotgun in relation to the body. Dr. Field had made it a point to explain the reaction of a man who has just been shot in the head. The victim is known to clutch something extremely tightly or throw it violently away. Pat had done neither, which implied the gun had been planted beside the body.

Although Dr. Field presented his findings in great detail before the Grand Jury, when it came time for the trial, "he wasn't questioned along these lines."[16]

Carl Adamson, on the other hand, was never called to appear in court. He and Miller had left the county before the case was called. Why was such bungling allowed? Why was Adamson, supposedly the only eye witness, allowed to leave?

As for Wayne Brazel, he continued to assert his innocence. He even "denied that Garrett was shot from behind." He told the court that Garrett came to him some days earlier and informed him [Brazel] that negotiations were underway to lease the land to Miller and Adamson. He further stipulated that he'd agreed to clear off the land provided Garrett could find a buyer for his goats at $3.50 a head.

Brazel even claimed, contrary to earlier reports, that he'd ridden all the way from the Garrett ranch house with Adamson and Garrett.

When questioned as to why he shot twice, Brazel replied that Adamson had hollered at him, "don't shoot him again." Brazel, however, claimed it was just reflex that caused him to fire the second bullet.

At 5:30 p.m., that same day, the jury was instructed to gather in private and return with their verdict. Fifteen minutes later they pronounced Jesse Wayne Brazel not guilty. Brazel was free. The plan had worked. Pat Garrett was dead and no one would suffer for his murder.

"Out on the Cox ranch there was a barbecue celebrating Brazel's acquittal. The celebration soon turned into an occasion of rejoicing over the passing of Pat Garrett," writes Keleher in *The Fabulous Frontier*.[17]

"Maybe the old-timers who thought Brazel took the rap for someone else were right!" Allen Papen told Ms. Hood. "There might have been a plot worked out by someone who didn't want to see Pat elected Sheriff...."

You've read the facts, gathered and presented in chronological order. "Does it sound like there may have been a fox in the henhouse?"

Quien Sabe!

The Worst Crime in New Mexico History

Before 1882, Bonito Canyon, New Mexico Territory was just another one of those lovely areas unmarred by "greedy civilization." However, in that year log cabins began to spring up about the canyon and the area quickly became known as Bonito City. Within no time at all merchants and men of various trades and professions moved into the area. The town soon boasted three general stores, a school, a saloon, a post office, a blacksmith shop, a lawyer's office, and a hotel.[1]

The Justice of the Peace, Charles Berry, boasted that his precinct had not had a single killing.

This boast didn't last long. Bonito City became the scene of a horrendous multiple murder which would be labeled as "the worst crime in New Mexico history...."

Martin Nelson was described by all who knew him as "a sane, good citizen who'd hailed from Nebraska" just four years earlier. The friendly young man quickly won the hearts and affection of the townspeople. As a result, they voted the youthful prospector their town constable.[2]

Nelson had a rented room in the Mayberry Hotel.[3] Also staying at the hotel was the town's new doctor, William H. Flynn, a recent arrival from Boston.

According to the newspaper, it was in the early morning hours when a noise awoke the doctor. He raised up in his bed and noticed Nelson sifting through his medical bag. He ordered Nelson to stop and leave his room at once.

Nelson went berserk.

Leveling his Winchester at the doctor, he fired point blank. He fired a second time. The doctor's body was thrown backwards against the wall and slumped to the floor — dead.

Worst Crime

The noise awoke the Mayberry family. Mr. Mayberry left his bed and went to the foot of the stairs to see what was happening. The door to the doctor's room burst open and Nelson ran out. He saw Mayberry.

Without any hesitation, Nelson pointed the rifle at Mayberry and fired a bullet into the man's chest. Mayberry's wife, standing nearby, heard the thump of lead as it found its way into her husband's body. She screamed.

Nelson aimed the rifle at her and pulled the trigger. She fell next to her husband — dead!

Nelson then stumbled downstairs. He ran into the room where the children slept. Loading another shell into the chamber, he squeezed the trigger. Now Mayberry's son was dead. Without any mercy, he next aimed the rifle at the little girl and pulled the trigger. Her young innocent body went limp.

By this time, Peter Nelson, the town grocer, had awakened to the sound of gunfire. He grabbed his sixgun and ran next door to the hotel. Without much caution, he entered the hotel and was met by Martin Nelson. It's not known if Peter and Martin were related. Recognizing Martin as the constable, Peter lowered his gun thinking all was well. As he did, Martin fired his rifle and shot Peter dead.

"All during the terror-stricken night," James Sherman relates in his book *Ghost Towns*, "the townspeople kept a close vigilance."

Toward sunrise the townspeople heard another shot. Several thought the murderer had committed suicide. But such was not to be. Instead, the saloonkeeper, Herman Beck, fell dead from a Winchester slug.

Nelson saw his chance to escape the hotel. He ran out the back door and toward the woods. He dodged from left to right as he continued to fire his Winchester. Reports differ as to exactly what happened next. The *Rio Grande Republican* reported he was killed by one of the townsfolk as he ran down the road. Sherman states that Charles Berry, the Justice of the Peace, tracked Martin into the woods and killed him. Whichever way it happened — Nelson was dead.

"The slain were buried," writes Sherman, "but the never-forgotten tragic episode of that night haunted the life of Bonito City."

Who knows, perhaps even today the ghosts of seven innocent victims still roam Bonito Canyon.

No Justice in the Old West

Two Mexican men brutally slaughtered several people in Las Cruces, New Mexico, including an innocent two year-old girl, in February, 1990. This event became known as the Las Cruces Bowl Massacre. Local authorities, unable to solve the crime, resorted to inviting Hollywood cameras to come to town and "re-create the crime for a well-known television show."[1] All it accomplished was to give the authorities national notoriety. As of this writing, the two men are still free.

In May, 1963, a man raped and murdered a New Mexico State University professor in her own back yard. The crime was "hushed-up from the start" and the murderer is still roaming free.[2]

Shortly after start of the year 1896, a prominent citizen of Mesilla, New Mexico Territory and his small son disappeared and their bodies never recovered. No one was ever punished for this crime.

These are but three of the many unsolved murders in southern New Mexico which, if they were all to be published, would fill a multi-volume encyclopedia.

Another of these unpunished murders occurred in 1877. The victim was the twenty-year old son of Mrs. Rooke, William Shepard. William's mother married Sergeant Rooke after the death of William's father.[3]

It was the night of September 28, 1877, and there were no clouds in the sky. The moon shone brightly over old Fort Tularosa, New Mexico Territory. Ten people, including William Shephard, gathered in the local boarding house. They were drinking, dancing, laughing, and merrymaking.

No Justice

A man named Overstreet started an argument with Shepard. The argument soon became a fist fight and William was knocked onto a nearby bed. Overstreet pulled a hunting knife he always carried and lunged at Shepard. The murderer's right arm went up into the air and forcibly came down seven brutal, slashing times into William's chest. William's body went limp. Blood splattered over the walls, ceiling, and floor. The bed sheets quickly soaked up the crimson fluid.

Overstreet lifted himself off the victim. He sheathed his knife, grabbed William by the nape of the neck and drug William's bloody corpse toward the front door. He opened the door and shoved the body outside.

"Either of the wounds would have been fatal," reported the newspaper.

Not one of the other eight people at the party bothered to interfere or attempted to stop the murder.

Lawman Patrick Higgins was notified and went directly to the house to investigate the crime. When he arrived, he found all nine people, including Overstreet, dancing and having a good time "as though nothing had ever happened."

He checked the bed and found it blood soaked. There was no doubt that a murder had taken place. He followed the trail of blood to the door and stepped outside to find William Shepard's body.

Higgins arrested Overstreet, who had "in his possession a large knife covered with blood and a pistol."

Overstreet spent the night in jail and was delivered up to the court the following day. Despite the fact that a Coroner's Jury "rendered a verdict to the effect that Shepard was killed by Overstreet," he was released and set free.

That newspaper reporter asked a question which continues to haunt New Mexicans, even today. "When will an example be made of men guilty of murder in New Mexico?"

WHEN?

Endnotes

Ghosts and Mysteries of the Old West
1. Murray, Earl. *Ghosts of the Old West*. Chicago: Contemporary Books, 1988.
2. *Las Cruces Sun-News*, Jan. 13, 1985. Las Cruces, NM.
3. Sherman, James. *Ghost Towns & Mining Camps of New Mexico* Norman: Univ. of Oklahoma Press, 1984.
4. Murray, *Ghosts*.
5. Sherman, *Ghost Towns*, p. 12.
6. Ibid.
7. Murray, *Ghosts*.
8. Sherman, *Ghost Towns*, pp. 224-226.
9. Ralph Looney, *Haunted Highways*, Hastings House, 1968, gives a different twist to the story. Both accounts are worth looking into by the serious-minded reader. The author, however, feels this account to be more accurate.
10. Murray, *Ghosts*.

A Town Born of Violence
1. Hallenbeck, Cleve. *Legends of the Spanish Southwest*. Glendale, CA: Arthur H. Clark Co., 1938.

Terror of the Sacramento Mountains
1. "Another Shooting Affray near La Luz," *Rio Grande Republican*, July 10, 1886.

Robbery at Paso del Norte
1. *Rio Grande Republican*, Dec. 22, 1883.
2. Gibson, A. M. *The Life and Death of Col. Albert J. Fountain*. Norman: Univ. of Oklahoma Press, 1965.

Saturday Night Lynching
1. *Rio Grande Republican*, May 1883.

Gunsmoke on Main Street
1. Gibson, *Life and Death*, p. 192.
2. A.J. Fountain to James Cree, Oct. 3, 1895. Fountain Papers, Univ. of Oklahoma Library.
3. Gibson, *Life and Death*, p. 214-18.
4. Behringer to Gibson, Feb. 18, 1961, Oklahoma City, OK.
5. Gibson, *Life and Death*, p. 217
6. Ibid., p. 208.
7. Ibid., p. 220.
8. *Rio Grande Republican*, Aug. 16, 1895.
9. Ben Michelson's Deposition, Las Cruces, N.M., Nov. 27, 1894. RG 60, NA.
10. Gibson, *Life and Death*, p. 206.
11. *Rio Grande Republican*, Aug-Oct 1895.
12. Ibid.
13. Ibid.

14. Gibson, *Life and Death*, p. 208.
15. *Rio Grande Republican*, Sept. 20, 1895.
16. "Albert Fall went before a grand jury and swore that the Stock Association had paid men to assassinate him...." "Williams was indicted for murder (killing a criminal he was attempting to arrest a year earlier)." Fountain, on the other hand, was indicted for "forging a private telegram to himself from Major Tell of El Paso some years before." A.M. Gibson, *Life and Death*, p. 225.
17. Sonnicheson, C.L.. *Tularosa: Last of the Frontier West*, Univ. of New Mexico Press, 1960. pp. 109, 309.

Old Buck's Ghost Still Roams New Mexico
1. Benton, Frank. *Cowboy Life on the Sidetrack* (Denver: The Western Stories Syndicate, 1930), cited in J. Frank Dobie, *A Vaquero of the Brush Country*. Dallas: The Southwest Press, 1929, pp. 165-166. Also in, *The Book of the American West*, Julian Messner, Inc., 1963, pp. 542-543.

Col. Fountain and the Twice Hung Man
1. Klasner, Lily Casey. *My Girlhood Among Outlaws*. Tucson: Univ. of Arizona Press, 1972.
2. Grubstake was a cowboy term for money which was generally used to buy food or "grub" to eat along the trail when traveling.
3. Klasner, *My Girlhood*.

The Black Coat Mystery
1. *Rio Grande Republican*, March 1885 gives Apodaca's testimony in great detail.
2. Looney, Ralph. *Haunted Highways*. Hastings House, 1968, p. 60.
3. *Rio Grande Republican*, Sept. 16, 1882 provides some details pertaining to the finding of the Nesmith wagon.
4. Meadows, John P. "Murder of the Nesmith Family," *Alamogordo News*, Aug. 15, 1935. See also: Philip Rasch, "The Nesmith Murder Mystery," *Denver Westerns Monthly Roundup*, Vol. 17, May 1961.

The Haunting Confession of Ruperto Lara
1. *Rio Grande Republican*, May 2, 1885.

Four Sevens and A Sixgun
1. Sherman, *Ghost Towns*, p. 182.
2. *Rio Grande Republican*, Jan. 6, 1883.

Shootout in Cotton's Saloon
1. Sherman, *Ghost Towns*, pp. 132-133.
2. *Rio Grande Republican*, Jan. 5, 1884.

Sin, Sex, and A Shooting!
1. *Rio Grande Republican*, May 12, 1883.

Col. Fountain and the Ghost of Ruidoso
1. Potter, Col. Jack, "Ruidoso, Ghost Steer of the Pecos," in *The Cattleman*, Ft. Worth, Vol. XXXVII (1950), p. 58-61. Also in James Monaghan, *The Book of the American West*, pp. 543-545.
2. See "Gunsmoke on Main Street for further details on this subject.
3. Gibson, *Life and Death*, pp. 229-231.
4. *The Book of the American West*, pp. 543-545.

The Ghost of Billy's Killer

1. Hood, Margaret P. "The Mysterious Death of Pat Garrett," *New Mexico Magazine*, Jan. 1957.
2. See "Col. Fountain and the Ghost of Ruidoso," for further details.
3. Gibson, *Life and Death*, p. 262.
4. Garrett, Pat. *The Authentic Life of Billy the Kid*. Norman: Univ. of Oklahoma Press, 1954, p. xiii.
5. Cline, Don. "Pat Garrett's Tragic Lawsuit," *Old West Magazine*, Summer 1989, pp. 18-23.
6. Metz, Leon. *Pat Garrett: The Story of A Western Lawman*. Norman: Univ. of Oklahoma Press, 1983, pp. 283-309.
7. Leon Metz, in his book about Garrett, doesn't believe this meeting ever took place. (p. 298) However, there are other reliable historians who do believe it took place. The account given here is taken from Metz's book. It is this author's opinion that the probability of such a "secret meeting" occurring is highly likely.
8. Mullin, Robert N. *The Strange Story of Wayne Brazel*. Canyon, TX: Palo Duro Press, 1969.
9. Hood, "Mysterious Death."
10. Metz, *Pat Garrett*, pp. 283-309. Also, Keleher, William. *The Fabulous Frontier*. Albuquerque: Univ. of N.M. Press, 1982, pp. 87-101.
11. George Turner, in his book *Gunfighters*, (Amarillo, TX: Baxter and Co., 1972) says, "Hardin was rolling dice with the bartender of the Acme Saloon, Henry Brown," (p. 37) when he was murdered by John Selmen, Jr.
12. This incident is given in detail by Metz in his book. Metz obtained the facts during an interview with Pauline Garrett, Las Cruces, NM, May 17, 1967.
13. Hood, "Mysterious Death."
14. Refer to the *Rio Grande Republican* coverage of the Garrett murder and trial - 1908-1909 issues. Also, great detail is given the trial by Leon Metz in his book.
15. Metz, *Pat Garrett*.
16. See Margaret P. Hood's article in the *New Mexico Magazine* for more details.
17. Keleher, *Fabulous Frontier*, p. 93.

The Worst Crime In New Mexico History

1. Sherman, *Ghost Towns*, p. 20.
2. *Rio Grande Republican*, May 9, 1885.
3. *The Rio Grande Republican* says M.S. Mayberry was the hotel owner. James Sherman gives the name as W.T. Mayberry. The newspaper indicates there were three children and Sherman says only two.

No Justice In the Old West

1. *Las Cruces Bulletin*, Feb-May 1990, Las Cruces, NM.
2. "Twas the Night Before Mother's Day," *Organ Mountain Trailblazer*, Vol. I, Issues 2&3, 1988. See also coverage of crime and cover-up in *Las Cruces Sun-New*, May-Dec 1963.
3. "A Foul Murder," *Mesilla Valley Independent*, Oct. 13, 1877.

Index

About the Author...

L'Aloge's writing has been described as "a breezy and colorful journalistic style, giving readers the feeling that they may have been moved back into the past."

He describes himself as a "real Westerner"; born and raised in southwestern Missouri—the home of Belle Starr, Jessie James and other Old West figures. L'Aloge pens his articles, stories and books with a flair and passion for historical detail and accuracy.

Of French-Irish descent, L'Aloge is proud of his heritage and the fact his ancestors fought for the **'Stars and Bars'** as well as **'Old Glory'**. He proudly volunteered and served in the United States Marine Corps during the Viet Nam War.

L'Aloge has lectured widely and his travels and research have taken him to 38 of the 50 states. His articles and short stories, plus a weekly column, have appeared in dozens of newspapers and magazines.

L'Aloge and son Joshua, currently live in Sparks, Nevada.

About the Illustrators...

Illustrator David Kwiecinski, although born in Ohio, has, developed roots in the desert southwest. As a small boy, Kwiecinski was introduced to this land, to its beauty, and to its history. Kwiecinski now resides in Las Cruces, NM. He received his B.F.A. degree from New Mexico State University and is now a practicing artist.

Marquita Peterson has lived in the southwest most of her life and currently lives in Albuquerque, New Mexico. Peterson's current emphasis is on historical Southwestern subjects and her "Southwest Legacies" series of sepia-toned ink drawings, reconstructed from tintypes and archival photos, shows a new depth of research and understanding of the Lincoln County War era.